INTRODUCTION

Introduction

Table of Contents:

Acknowledgments

Thank you to all who contributed to the creation of this guidebook. Your insights and contributions are incredibly valuable and highly appreciated. This book could not have happened without your unending support!

University of Michigan School for Environment and Sustainability (SEAS)
Special acknowledgment given to the Behavior, Education and Communication department and Environmental Psychology Lab within SEAS, as well as the Resilience Project.

Farm Stop Owners/Managers:
Adam Schweiterman and Jessica Eikelberry- Local Roots
Ruth VanBogelen - Acorn Farmer's Market and Café
Hillary Melville and Robin Mullaney - Random Harvest
Emily Watson - Boone Street Market
Shelly Keeney - The Wild Ramp

Editors and Contributors:
Kathy Sample - Argus Farm Stop
Katy Alexander - ZingTrain at Zingerman's
Raymond De Young - Academic Advisor, SEAS

Graphic Design Team:
Valerie Le - Formatting
Beatrice Miller - Graphics and Cover Art

Overview

Farm Stops are year-round, every-day markets that support small-scale farmers and strengthen local and regional food systems. They do so most often by operating on a consignment model, which gives producers a fair price, flexibility with their time and products, and provides more direct connections with consumers. This document briefly outlines the need for Farm Stops, then offers a comprehensive, but not definitive, guide to the essential components required to develop a Farm Stop.

Context

In the United States, more than 2.02 million farms operate nation-wide (USDA, 2022). 89 percent of these farms are small-scale family farms grossing less than $350,000 annually, and account for only 20 percent of total food production. By contrast, large-scale farms exceeding one million dollars annually account for 3 percent of farms, yet produce over 45 percent of total food production (USDA, 2022). These large-scale farms typically use highly industrialized and conventional agricultural methods to produce raw materials for further processing, or produce large quantities of meat and dairy products. These raw materials include corn, soy, cotton, and other grain products and are typically processed into feed for livestock, biofuels such as ethanol, or sweeteners and preservatives found in packaged foods. As small-scale family farms continue to decline, the average farm size increases (USDA, 2017; USDA, 2022). Furthermore, 95 percent of farmers are older males who are quickly retiring (Reiley and Van Dam, 2019), leaving large gaps in agricultural knowledge and practice for upcoming generations. Lastly, economic and weather-related challenges, including drought and hurricanes, have kept production costs high for vegetable, livestock, and dairy farmers, making it increasingly difficult for them to make a living

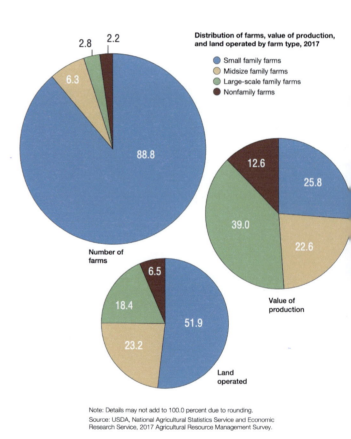

Figure 1: Distribution of Farms, Value of Production, and Land Operated by Farm Type, 2017.

(Johansson, 2020). These statistics reveal the current climate of our national food system: decades of consolidation of large-scale farms and increasing homogeneity. This homogenized system has increased large-scale conventional farmers' reliance on middle-men supply chains.

Within our current industrial food system, farmers on average only receive approximately 16 cents for every dollar of goods sold through wholesale or retail channels, leaving the majority of their profits and hard work supporting those middlemen supply chains (USDA, 2022b). Additionally, small scale farmers make the majority of their profits through direct-to-consumer sales through farmer's markets and Community Supported Agriculture (CSA) programs, which account for 8 percent of food purchases in the country. This leaves 92 percent of food purchased indirectly from middlemen supply chains, which further accelerates the decline of small-scale farms (USDA, 2022a).

When the COVID-19 pandemic hit the United States in March of 2020, it sparked a wave of national and state government shutdowns and stay-at-home orders that altogether halted the economy, and left this homogenized system scrambling. While many businesses and economic sectors floundered during this time, the agricultural sector was forced to continue operating as it was, and still is, necessary and essential. During this period, farms of all sizes experienced a number of challenges and changes that created mixed results in their efficiency at feeding the nation. These challenges included severe labor shortages, increased demand for fresh food, lack of viable economic outlets, and large quantities of food waste (Borman et al., 2020; Clapp, 2020; Lush, 2020; Lakhani, 2020; Poppick, 2020; Yaffe-Bellany and Corkery, 2020). The COVID-19 pandemic has, if anything else, highlighted the fragility of our current food system, and has forced us to question alternative, more sustainable systems for future generations.

We are **vulnerable**
in this industrial food system.

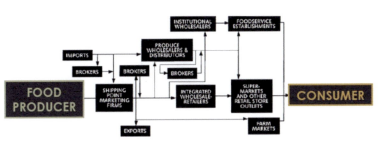

- Travels long distances – on average 1500 miles
- Dependent on fossil fuels
- Vulnerable to climate change, oil shortages, aquifers, and other disruptions (like COVID-19).

- Direct connection between producer and consumer
- Producers make more money, because no middlemen or distributors
- Limited availability due to weather, seasonality, and lack of convenient locations to purchase

Source: USDA Census of Agriculture, 2017

Figure 2: Graphic representation of middle-men supply chains vs. direct-to-consumer sales provided by the Argus Farm Stop 3-Day Online Course.

Small-Farm Supporting Grocery Stores: Farm Stops

One such system is a regional or local food economy. This economy not only supports small-scale local farmers implementing sustainable agricultural practices that use fewer fossil fuels (USDA, 2017), but they also reduce carbon emissions associated with food transportation by sourcing food within a smaller geographic range. Lastly, this system minimizes reliance on national supply chains, thereby enhancing community resilience to global crises such as national economic recessions and pandemics.

To strengthen regional and local food economies, I turn to the Small-Farm Supporting Grocery Store, otherwise known as a Farm Stop. These stores are mission-driven and prioritize supporting and enabling small-scale producers by sourcing directly within a specified local radius. They further perpetuate this mission of supporting small-scale producers by implementing a specific business model based on consignment, which ensures that producers get the real value of their products. Most people, when they hear the word, 'consignment,' immediately think of clothing, or antique stores. But this model has important implications for supporting small-scale producers and strengthening local food systems. For example, Argus Farm Stop in Ann Arbor, Michigan is a year-round Small-Farm Supporting Grocery store that works with over 200 local farmers and producers. They give their producers 70 percent of the retail price, and take a 30 percent commission of those sales to maintain operations.

With stores like the Argus Farm Stop, producers set their own prices, own their products until they are sold, and make more money than an average retail sale. This not only gives small-scale farmers a fair price year-round, but it also allows them to preserve their identity, and have an additional year-round direct-to-consumer outlet. Since opening in 2014, Argus Farm Stop has put over $10 million back into the hands of small-scale producers. In addition to strengthening the local food economy, stores like Argus Farm Stop foster closer relationships with the producers they work with, educate others about the benefits of eating locally and seasonally, and enhance creativity and expression in a community. In this way, Farm Stops help strengthen local food economies, educate consumers about the benefits of local food, and build community.

The name, Farm Stop, was first coined by Argus Farm Stop in 2014. It was chosen because this particular model is at once a farmer's market, a farm stand, and a regular retail operation. It combines elements from each to provide a supportive place for local, small-scale producers to "stop" and sell their goods, and have a cup of coffee while chatting with customers. From here on out, I'll explain how you can build your own version of a Farm Stop in your community.

How to Use This Document

This document is a variation of a Pattern Language, which was established by Christopher Alexander in 1977 to highlight the behavioral and psychological interactions in urban and architectural design (Alexander et al., 1977). Pattern Languages consist of a series of patterns that identify a specific element, situation, or challenge of a built environment; and, offer suggested tips and solutions to address it. Often, patterns are interrelated.

For the purpose of this document, each pattern highlights a specific element involved in developing Farm Stops, and offers suggested solutions and resources gleaned from successful iterations of existing Farm Stops. Patterns are organized within sections: Getting Started, Financials, Location, Communication, and Operations. At the end of each pattern is a list of related patterns. This allows for a more fluid and interactive experience in which the reader may flip back and forth between these pages to pick and choose the patterns that pertain most to where they are in developing their store. All resources within each pattern are included at the end of this document in the Resources and References section.

While this document is comprehensive, it is not exhaustive. Some topics are not fully covered, or are excluded entirely. I am open to receiving feedback and suggestions about how to improve this resource. If you wish to add further information about a certain topic, or would like to include additional topics, feel free to contact me directly at **katbarr@umich.edu.**

Summary

This document is meant to guide and encourage the creation and development of Farm Stops, similar to that of **Argus Farm Stop** in Ann Arbor, Michigan. For those interested in developing a Farm Stop in their community, this document will not only highlight some of the most essential elements, but it will also help you map out exactly how you want your store to look, feel, and operate. In addition to highlighting the most essential elements, this guide offers resources to help you achieve your goal. I hope you find these pages useful.

GETTING STARTED

Mission

Utility: Before you do anything else to develop your own Farm Stop, take a minute to consider your mission statement. Your mission statement is a summation of your store's intention, goals and priorities within your community. Mission statements can describe a set list of values or principles you aim to uphold, as well as who you are as a company. Overall, this statement lets people in your community know who you are, what you do, and what you stand for.

Context: Having a clear, concise mission statement not only helps to define your business within the context of your community, but it also helps you solidify your vision and thus aid in the development of the finer details of your store. In doing so, your mission statement ensures your store aligns with your values, helps you attract like-minded staff and investors, and overall helps to maintain (or even expand) your operations.

When drafting your mission statement, consider the following questions:

Who do you want to be as a company?
For example:
- Are you a non-profit, a worker or member owned co-op, an L3C?
- Are you a resource for community development?

What is it you hope to achieve in your community?
For example:
- Do you want to grow your local economy?
- Support small-scale farmers?
- Strengthen the resilience of your community?
- Create additional jobs?
- Collaborate with and support other local businesses?

What is it you stand for?
For example:
- Are you passionate about supporting labor rights?
- About sourcing local foods?
- About strengthening your community by providing an inclusive space?

Your mission statement may contain any, all or none of the ideas mentioned above (See Table 1: Mission Statement) and can be as long or as short as you like; but it must be uniquely tailored to your personal reasoning for developing a Farm Stop and the values you hope to instill in your community.

Table 1: Mission Statements of Existing Farm Stops

Argus Farm Stop, Ann Arbor, MI	The Wild Ramp Huntington, WV	Random Harvest Craryville, NY	Local Roots, Wooster, OH
"Our mission is to grow our local agricultural economy. How? We want small, local farms to succeed. We provide a place where local farms can sell locally-grown produce and other goods conveniently to consumers, year-round!"	"The Wild Ramp (Tri-State Local Foods, Inc.) is a year-round, non-profit farmers market based in Huntington, West Virginia, with a mission to grow and support a vibrant economy and community for local food, food products, and artisan goods."	"Random Harvest is a worker-owned neighborhood market, cafe, and community space that: provides food and goods sourced directly from farmers and producers; brings together diverse community for shared work, sustenance, and learning; and uses models of exchange, pricing, and ownership to reflect the needs of workers, producers, and community members."	"We are a vibrant Co-op that features seasonal, sustainable foods and art from more than 200 local producers. We connect the community with environmentally and socially responsible businesses locally, regionally, and globally."

Additional Resources: For additional resources on drafting mission statements, see *Resources, Mission.*

Related Patterns: Financials - Business Structure, Financials - Wholesale Options, Financials - Community Partnerships, Financials - Community Events as Fundraisers, Financials - Donations and Crowd-Sourcing, Financials - Educational Classes and Community Events, Communications - Marketing

FINANCIALS

Financials

Overview: Financials are one of the most important and difficult aspects of developing your store. This chapter will cover everything from how to organize your business structure, to finding the right funding mechanisms, to knowing which forms of diversified revenue are best for your particular model, and much more.

Table of Contents:

For additional resources on planning financials, see: *Resources, Financials* at end.

Business Structure

Utility: Business Structure determines how your store makes money, how you present your store to the community, and most importantly, how you pay taxes and are exposed to liability. Here's where you decide whether you want to be for-profit or non-profit.

Context: This is one of the first steps in starting any business and it is highly advised that you consult with tax and legal professionals.

Visit the Small Business Administration (SBA) to learn more about **the right business structure for you**, and to **find local representatives in your area** that may help you in this process.

Please note that the availability of specific business structures in your region is often dependent on state regulations, which require specific state or city permits to file. Visit the SBA to find local agents to help you sort out your options.

There are many other resources that exist in addition to those listed on the SBA. For example, check your state's local networks and universities. For example, Michigan has the **Michigan Small-Business Development Center,** which offers an immense network of resources for those starting small businesses; and the University of Michigan has myriad resources for entrepreneurship and financial planning.

The most pertinent business structures for Farm Stops include the following:

Low profit, limited liability company (L3C)
- This option is only available in some states. If your state does not offer the option of forming an L3C, a B-Corporation is a good alternative.
- An L3C ensures that the organization operates under for-profit financial practices, and focuses primarily on funding their mission instead of the owners.

B-Corporation
- This option is similar to an L3C as it is driven by mission and profit. Shareholders hold the company accountable to producing profits and a public benefit.

Limited liability company (LLC)
- This option offers protection to the owner(s) from personal liability for debts and other potential obligations a business might incur.

Non-profit corporation
- This option is exempt from federal income tax under section 501(c)(3) of Title 26 of the United States Code.

Cooperative
- Your cooperative could be organized as member owned or worker owned.
- Please note that any Cooperative structure requires a board of directors and other operating organizations that may require additional resources.

Now, what's the difference between each structure and why choose one over the other?

See Table 2, cited from the Small Business Association, to understand the foundational differences between your options. Please note that some business structures are not included in this chart. For additional information about these entities, such as L3Cs, please speak with a trusted financial advisor.

Table 2: Business Structures

Business structure	Ownership	Liability	Taxes
Sole proprietorship	One person	Unlimited personal liability	Self-employment tax Personal tax
Partnerships	Two or more people	Unlimited personal liability unless structured as a limited partnership	Self-employment tax (except for limited partners) Personal tax
Limited liability company (LLC)	One or more people	Owners are not personally liable	Self-employment tax Personal tax or corporate tax
Corporation - C corp	One or more people	Owners are not personally liable	Corporate tax
Corporation - S corp	One or more people, but no more than 100, and all must be U.S. citizens	Owners are not personally liable	Personal tax
Corporation - B corp	One or more people	Owners are not personally liable	Corporate tax
Corporation - Nonprofit	One or more people	Owners are not personally liable	Tax-exempt, but corporate profits can't be distributed

(United States Small Business Administration)

It is important to keep in mind how each business structure approaches governance. Co-ops have elected boards and are communal, which sometimes pose additional decision-making challenges as many points of view need to be considered. Non-profits also require an external board of directors. They need to balance the responsibility of the board, and how much is delegated to store management. Within an LLC, the owners make decisions based on operational and retail demands.

Once you have settled on a specific business structure, **register your business with the SBA.**

Additional Resources: For a list of resources referenced in this pattern, see *Resources, Business Structure.*

Related Patterns: Financials - Funding Mechanisms, Financials - Grants, Financials - Private Funds, Financials - Donations and Crowd-Sourcing, Financials - Loans, Financials - Social Programs: SNAP/EBT

Consignment Ratios

Utility: Most retail grocery stores operate by reselling the producer's goods. Most existing Farm Stops, however, implement their version of a consignment model to ensure that the small-scale farmers and producers they work with receive the real price of their goods. It also preserves the relationship between customers and farmers.

Context: Consignment ratios determine the percentage of the retail price the producer and the store each receive. For example, the standard consignment ratio for several existing Farm Stops is currently 75 (farmer) / 25 (Farm Stop), where the producer receives 75 percent of the retail price of all goods sold, and the store receives 25 percent. This helps organize sales and inventory, ensure your bottom line, and also aids in developing producer relationships.

This ratio is a major selling point when recruiting farmers and producers to sell at your store. Remember: on average, American farmers make 16 cents of the customer dollar spent in a retail operation. So the percentage they receive through this ratio is much higher than what they would receive in a typical retail or wholesale transaction. This ratio can also offset the labor and time costs of participating in one-day-a-week farmer's markets.

Consignment ratios are determined by what your store needs to sustain your finances. This ensures you have funds available for maintenance or operational needs, and often requires crunching some numbers before you settle on your ratio. For example, a 75/25 ratio may sound great, but might not be sustainable for keeping the lights on in the long run. When estimating your finances, consider the following:

Table 3: Choosing the right consignment ratio

What Are You Selling?	When Are You Selling It?	Who is Selling It?	How Are You Selling It?	Rental Payments and Utilities	Credit Card Processing Fees
See *Types of Goods*	See *Receiving and Accessibility*	See *Payroll and Staffing*	See *Diversified Revenue*	See *Location*	See *Point of Sale System*

You don't have to choose one consignment ratio for all goods. For example, Local Roots in Wooster, Ohio charges different consignment ratios based on the goods sold; farmers and producers receive 82 percent of the retail price for all produce, baked goods and milk, but 75 percent for frozen foods, eggs and dairy. Consignment ratios are flexible, so long as you communicate any changes with your producers.

Important Caveats: It is very important to consider the consignment ratio you start with! Make sure this reflects your ability to pay staff and operate sustainably over time, especially if you plan to add additional services such as an online store or subscription service (See *Diversified Revenue*). For example, several Farm Stops found that an 80/20 ratio is not financially sustainable.

Be careful! The more complex your ratio, the more staff and operations are required to maintain it. Local Roots has to ensure that they keep adequate records of all producers with their specific ratio, bill each producer correctly, monitor inventory and maintain adequate communication. That all adds up, especially if you have a large number of producers.

Additional Resources: For an example spread-sheet of how to estimate your expenses and determine your consignment ratio, see *Resources, Consignment Ratios*.

Related Patterns: Financials - Wholesale Options, Communication - Producer Relationships, Financials - Sources of Additional and Higher Margin Income, Operations - Types of Goods, Operations - Hours and Accessibility, Operations - Payroll and Staffing, Location - Location, Operations - Point of Sale System

Wholesale Options

Utility: Utility: Some stores offer producers the option of operating on a wholesale agreement instead of selling on consignment. While this is possible, reserve this for items that go through distributors or are critical for your every-day market such as milk. Mixing wholesale and consignment is difficult to track and difficult for employees to understand. Plus, if your mission is to grow the local food economy, the best way to do so is through direct-to-consumer sales. Producers may want a wholesale agreement for a number of reasons including:

1. The producer cannot handle selling their goods via consignment.
2. Sometimes, larger-sized producers have a hard time managing their inventory if they sell by consignment.
3. Accountants also have a hard time tracking items sold by consignment
4. Diversified revenue avenues, such as a café, may require larger quantities of products that are more frequently consumed (ex. Bread, milk, coffee). This can change your relationship with specific producers as the demand for their products is higher and more consistent, and relies on the producer's ability to monitor inventory. As a result, it may be easier to purchase these items wholesale, or from a regional distributor.
5. Some stores have commercial kitchens that sell prepared meals using goods from producers that also sell in the store. Wholesale may better facilitate taking producers' product from the store shelves into the kitchen.
6. Some stores start off strong recruiting producers, but over time found that recruiting became more difficult, especially for specific goods. Offering wholesale options can be a good way to recruit more producers, and potentially increase the diversity of your offerings.

Regional Distributors: Many Farm Stops may look to establish a wholesale relationship with a regional distributor. This can be useful for the following:

1. Certain items may not be locally available such as oils, grains, flours, chips or other staple and processed goods. This is dependent on your store's mission and whether you want to offer such products, as well as by demand in your location.
2. When certain items that are typically available locally, such as spinach, suddenly become unavailable due to a difficult growing season or other logistical difficulties. This requires strong communication with your producers to determine whether it is a good idea to replace these items via regional distributors for a specific period of time during the season to meet demand for that product.
3. Some stores find it more difficult to recruit producers for specific goods. Seeking out regional distributors is often a solution to this problem.

Context: Stores do not have to offer a wholesale option, but it can help to:

- Diversify your offerings and enhance a more complete shopping experience.
- Enhance the efficiency of your diversified revenue operation.
- Serve as a useful backup if necessary items become unavailable.

Distributors work on a number of different scales from national to regional to hyper-local. The best method to find a distributor that best aligns with your mission is to either conduct a google search to find distributors in your area, or to ask around and see if other local food businesses have recommendations.

Caveats: When working with regional distributors consider the following:

- Make sure that working with a regional distributor does not violate your Mission statement, or the ethics of your store. It is essential that you are as transparent as possible about which products come from regional distributors, and why you chose to work with them. Never mislead your customers, or offend your producers!
- Using regional distributors in place of seeking out additional producers is often a slippery slope to losing the consignment model entirely. It is best to carefully pick and choose exactly how you wish to engage with a regional distributor, and for what products.
- Make sure you create the ways in which you will manage wholesale products in addition to consignment products. For example, have confidence in addressing how you will maintain inventory, or how you will respond to price increases from the distributor.

Table 4: Regional Food Distributors used by Existing Farm Stops

Argus Farm Stop Ann Arbor, MI	Random Harvest Craryville, NY	Boone Street Market Jonesborough, TN
• **Cherry Capital** • **Frog Holler**	• **Hudson Harvest** • **Baldor** • **Associated Buyers** • **Farms2Tables** • **Marty's Local** • **Regional Access** • **Mable**	• **Southern Culture** • **Blue Mountain**

Additional Resources: For the links to each regional distributor, see *Resources, Wholesale Options.*

Related Patterns: Financials - Consignment Ratios, Operations - Producer Information, Communication - Producer Relationships

Funding Mechanisms

Utility: Funding for start-up and maintenance costs is arguably the most challenging aspect of developing a Farm Stop.

To better understand your costs, first identify a location and consider your initial staffing needs. Staffing needs are among the highest costs Farm Stops incur. Having this information in place can help you to determine the primary costs and resources necessary for store-build out and maintenance, and can provide a clearer picture for how and where to procure the funds you need.

For more information on staffing needs and examples, visit *Payroll and Staffing*. See also *Location*.

Context: Before you create a fundraising campaign on social media or start writing grants, consider estimating the finances you need to build and maintain your store within the first 3-5 years, as most consignment-based grocery stores do not break even within the first year. These estimates and projections can help give you a better sense of how much money you need to raise, and what financial avenues will best help you to reach your goals.

Common Fundraising Methods Include:
- Grants
- Private Funds
- Community Partnerships
- Community Events as Fundraisers
- Donations and Crowd-Sourcing
- Loans

The most common and successful forms of fundraising for existing Farm Stops include Community Partnerships, and Crowd-Sourcing.

Related Patterns: Financials - Grants, Financials - Private Funds, Financials - Community Partnerships, Financials - Community Events as Fundraisers, Financials - Donations and Crowd-Sourcing, Financials - Loans, Financials - Sources of Additional and Higher Margin Income, Location - Demographics.

Table 5: Suggested Steps to Estimate Your Store's Finances

Scout out your location to get an idea of foot traffic.

This provides a baseline estimate of average customers you may anticipate receiving per day if 100 percent of passersby stop in your store. You can, of course, change the estimated percentage of customers per day to meet a certain goal, such as 20 customers per day.

Your local Small Business Development Center can also provide demographics and traffic studies for your location.

Estimate anticipated average sales per customer.

This refers to how much you would want each customer to spend when they visit your store.

Estimate average daily, monthly and yearly sales.

Use your customers per day and your average sales to calculate this. When doing so, don't forget to subtract your consignment ratio as the cost of goods sold.

Calculate your total gross sales.

Use Steps 2 and 3 for all additional income sources as well, such as a cafe, to find your total gross sales. Remember to also subtract the anticipated cost of goods sold in the cafe to get your total monthly or yearly estimate from your diversified revenue.

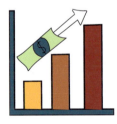

Analyze your baseline.

Add up the gross totals between the market and any additional income outlets, and use this number as a baseline for how to plan your finances, especially for the first three years.

Additional Resources: For sample spead-sheets illustrating how to estimate your expenses, income, and start-up costs see *Resources, Funding Mechanisms.*

Grants

Utility: Grants are a useful tool to getting funds for your business, and there are many that exist on a state and national level to offer support.

Context: While grants can be a wonderful way to get funding, there are many important considerations to be aware of before prioritizing grants as your primary form of fund-raising:

- They are highly competitive and rely on specific timelines.
  - Make sure grant timelines align with your needs so you do not waste time on inaccessible opportunities.
- They often require a lot of time and labor, especially if you do not have prior experience in grant-writing. If you have the resources available to do so, it may be worth seeking out someone who has grant-writing experience.
- The world of available grants is vast and difficult to navigate. See *Resources, Grants* for USDA grant listings specifically available to food producers.
- Finding the right grants requires an additional level of time and labor as deadlines often move quickly, and new grants are often not well advertised.

Federal grants typically offer larger sums of money, and are more widely advertised; but are highly competitive and often have strict regulations and reporting requirements that may limit their usefulness. These applications take a lot of time and preparation to meet specified requirements. Do not underestimate the time and skill required to apply for these opportunities.

State level grant funds will vary, but they may be more accessible as competition is lower, and they may not have as stringent requirements as national grants. Check your state's **Department of Agriculture** as they often offer grant opportunities. For example, The Michigan Department of Agriculture and Rural Development is the primary state-level grantor for the state of Michigan.

Grants.gov is a comprehensive website aimed to help individuals and organizations not only find the right grant for their needs, but also provides tools and resources to aid in completing your applications. Other resources include the **Michigan State University Center for Regional Food Systems' Funding Sources for Food-Related Businesses: Sixth Edition.**

Your business structure can also help you identify opportunities your business is most eligible to apply for. Non-profits, for example, are often eligible for a variety of grants, while Co-Ops may not be. Be sure to understand your business structure, and how it impacts grant eligibility.

Additional Resources: For a list of USDA Federal Grant Programs, and Non-Federal Grant databases, see *Resources, Grants*.

Related Patterns: Financials - Funding Mechanisms, Financials - Business Structure

Private Funds

Utility: It's worth noting that few small business owners start without some skin in the game. Many Farm Stop owners invest at least some of their own personal money into their business, or create personal networks of family and friends who are willing to invest.

Context: It is recommended that you budget your own personal accounts in a safe and productive manner with the help of certified professionals.

Asking Friends and Family for Investments:

If you have a great idea, chances are others will think so too. Asking friends and family to invest in your idea is common for many start-ups. Before pitching your idea, it is important to consider the nature of your relationships with friends and family, as this can impact the nature of the investment.

While the agreement depends on the nature of your relationship, it is highly recommended that you facilitate a more formal interaction. For example, it is a good idea to consult a legal professional and have them draw up a business investment or loan agreement with specified repayment terms. In addition, it is important to understand the difference between an active investor and a passive investor.

You could also consider offering equity in the business in exchange for their financial support. In this case, it is recommended that you consult a legal professional to draw up formal contracts and paperwork that specify and define the terms and conditions of the agreement.

If this is your preferred option, consider how much equity you offer and the details of that equity, including how much decision-making power you offer. The amount of equity offered also has the potential to affect your relationships, so try to maintain as much individual control within any friends and family transactions as possible.

To determine how best to arrange your personal finances, speak with a local banking, business or legal professional, and talk to as many local organizations or small business owners as possible. The more people you talk to, the more tools and resources you'll have at your disposal.

Related Patterns: Financials - Funding Mechanisms

Community Partnerships

Utility: Community partnerships are not only a great way to raise funds for your store, but they also help to further embed your store in the community, and serve as everlasting resources.

Context: Community partnerships can take on many forms depending on the purpose of the partnership. There are financial partnerships, community-oriented partnerships, and educational partnerships, among others.

The more partnerships you have, the more ingrained you will be in your community. The more ingrained you are in your community, the more credible your reputation becomes, and the more locals and visitors alike recognize and support your store.

More importantly, generating community partnerships offers an opportunity to educate others about your mission and foster opportunities to understand how your store can best serve your community. This helps to elevate your store's value in your community, and will help you to find others who align with your mission.

Here are three ways to establish community partnerships:

1. Consider first and foremost partnering with your city commissioner or governing offices to develop a healthy working relationship with them. This relationship is especially useful in the event you need to perform any construction or expansions.

2. Shop around your community to find organizations that align with your mission so that you can host events together, sponsor each other, or support each other in other ways.

3. Make a list of all local or regional organizations or businesses you already know of, then ask around your community to learn of others.
   - Reach out to organizations that enhance the accessibility of your store to all populations within the community.
   - These businesses and organizations may want to make use of your space, or partner for community events - even if no money is involved! This helps spread awareness of your image and mission, and further engrains you into the culture of your community.

Table 6: Examples of Community Partnerships from existing Farm Stops

Argus Farm Stop, MI

Engaged in non-financial conversations with the City of Ann Arbor to demonstrate the public good of refurbishing abandoned buildings, since their primary location used to be an old gas station.

Partnered with nearby colleges/universities to collaborate with research projects related to supporting regional food systems.

Local Roots, OH

Partnered with the City Commissioner to use their current building rent-free.

Partnered with nearby colleges/universities to collaborate with research projects related to supporting regional food systems.

Random Harveest, NY

Partnered with organizations that helped improve equitable accessibility of their store by enhancing distribution of Farm Stop products to low-income residents.

The Wild Ramp, WV

Partnered with numerous local businesses and organizations to create a handout of weekly and monthly community events, posted around the store.

Boone Street Market, TN

Partnered with the Jonesborough outdoor farmers market to generate further interest and support for both the store and market.

Each of these are valuable contributions to the health and well-being of your community. The more you engage in these activities, the more you increase the value of your store.

Farm Stops typically exist to support their communities. The more you show up for your community, the more your community will show up for you!

Related Patterns: Financials - Community Partnerships, Financials - Community Events as Fundraisers, Financials - Educational Classes and Community Events, Location - Community Demographics

Community Events as Fundraisers

Utility: Community events can be an integral part of your fundraising plan and can take on a number of different forms. Not only can they help raise money for your store, but they are also a great way to strengthen Community Partnerships and build trust and value for your store in your community. Lastly, they can help you better connect with the thought leaders of your community.

Context: Examples of community events existing Farm Stops have hosted include:
- Farm-to-table dinners featuring their producers' products
  - For events like these, you can look into collaborating with local chefs or restaurants, food trucks, or other local food businesses
- Collaborations with other local events such as food summits or Community Supported Agriculture fairs.
- Concerts with local musicians
- Art fairs featuring local artists
  - This is especially useful if you decide to sell craft goods.
- Tasting events featuring your producers' goods.
- Movie screenings that relate to your store's mission
- Block parties that celebrate the diversity of businesses in your immediate area.
  - This helps people familiarize themselves with where you are in the community and further strengthens Community Partnerships

These events are meant to be fun, inclusive, relaxing and enjoyable for the whole community and can coincide with other holidays, goals, and seasonal festivals to create a theme, or amp up participation. For example, seasonal festivals, particularly in the summer or fall, can really help to showcase your producers' products and what your store has to offer.

It goes without saying, however, that organizing events requires a lot of time, effort and funding itself, especially if you are organizing your event with multiple community partners. This can make the event-planning process seem overwhelming. When organizing community events, remember that you have full control over the size, duration, and necessary materials.

Here are some tips to get you started:

- Set a firm budget on how much you are willing to spend on necessary time, labor and materials such as tables, chairs, audio/visual equipment, decorations etc.
  - Know exactly what you need, how many people will be required to set it up and take it down, and how long the event will take, not just on the day itself but in the weeks leading up to the event.
- Create a schedule with due dates and deadlines.
  - This is especially important if your event requires many moving parts that may be difficult to keep track of.
- Make sure you have help. You don't need to do this alone! It can sometimes take a village to create a fun and memorable experience, but that doesn't mean you as the organizer have to miss out.
  - Take advantage of as many Community Partnerships as possible.
  - Create regularly scheduled meetings or check-in points with your team to ensure everything is going smoothly.
- Use tools and technology if available.
  - Planning and organizational tools such as Google Docs, Gantt Charts, **Mural**, **Miro**, **Trello** or even **Excel Event Planning Templates** not only helps to organize all the fine details, but also ensures you and your team are on the same page.
- Remember to have fun with the process!

Additional Resources: For links to planning and organization tools, see *Resources, Community Events as Fundraisers.*

Related Patterns: Financials - Community Partnerships

Donations and Crowd-Sourcing

Utility: A smaller, but effective method for raising funds is appealing to your customers and community for individual donations made in person or online. Asking for individual donations also facilitates conversations about your store's mission and purpose in the community. This may help customers better connect with you, support you, and even spread the word to get more donations.

Context: While individual donations are usually small with most occurring in $5 increments, generating enough can really help to support your financial goals. While these amounts may seem small, never underestimate the power of your community.

While crowd-sourcing campaigns reap big rewards for many, know that they often require more time and effort to organize and maintain. Try to seek out others who have experience in crowd-sourcing, or look at current Farm Stops that have had success with this method such as The Wild Ramp in Huntington, West Virginia and Acorn Farmer's Market and Café in Manchester, Michigan.

Please note that if you plan on crowd-sourcing, you must keep your business structure in mind, and any regulatory fiduciary controls of where the money is held. If you register as a 501c3 non-profit, you are able to steward your own money. If you register as an LLC, L3C, or a B-Corp, you may need a third-party vendor, such as **Patronicity**, or another 501c3 non-profit to act as the holding entity for the money you collect. At the very least, you will need a fiduciary plan that shows the money you collect is going to an approved, organized, legal entity.

Asking for donations requires a lot of community outreach, so always be as transparent as possible with your community about the reason you are asking for donations, and what the money will be used for. Whether the donations are just for general upkeep and operational maintenance of your store, or if the funds are going to a major expansion project, make sure your community knows where their money is going to and for what.

Table 7: Tips and tricks to foster donations

Use Levels	Offer Perks or Rewards	Use Free Graphic Design Platforms	Be as Concise as Possible
Offer people the option to donate different amounts.	Rewards can potentially encourage higher donations. Rewards include anything from a free ticket to classes or workshops you may host, to products from local producers you will feature at the store, to store merchandise, if this is within your budget.	When creating materials to encourage participating in your donation fund, free graphic design platforms such as **Canva** have many ready-made templates to choose from.	If you are asking for donations on social media or other online platforms, remember to only include one call to action at a time as too much information can be overwhelming.

Table 8: Ways to facilitate donations for your store

The Tried and True Method

For those with store-fronts, this involves setting out traditional donation boxes or jars at the checkout counter or around the store.

For those without storefronts, post fliers around your community, and use your Community Partnerships to ask other local businesses to advertise your funding campaign. Be sure to include on the flier how they may donate to your fund.

Try to make boxes and fliers colorful, eye-catching, and succinct.

This method also offers the option of asking customers to donate when they make a purchase.

Websites

If you already have a website for your business, a landing page, or even a personal website, adding a donation button or a pop-up screen on the homepage can help encourage donations.

Even if you don't include these direct methods of payment via your website, you can simply post information about your fundraiser and where to donate.

Email

If your store includes a newsletter, or if you have access to community listservs, use these as resources to tell people about your store, your fundraiser and your mission. Be sure that you have permission to access any community listservs, and not to abuse any private information.

Social Media

Take advantage of social media platforms such as Instagram, TikTok, and Facebook to ask for donations, or to alert followers of an ongoing donation fund.

This method is also useful for those who may not yet have a website.

Crowd-Sourcing

Remember to be aware of your business structure, and the importance of wording. See *Resources, Donations and Crowd-Sourcing* for articles related to suggested wording for crowd-soucing campaigns. The following platforms can act as the holding entity when collecting money, and can also help to organize contacting people via listservs:

- **GoFundMe**
- **Indiegogo**
- **Kickstarter**
- **Patronicity**

Additional Resources: For links of the resources provided in this section, see *Resources, Donations and Crowd-Sourcing.*

Related Patterns: Financials - Business Structure, Financials - Community Partnerships, Communication - Marketing.

Loans

Utility: While most people want to avoid having to take out loans, many Farm Stops have benefitted from using them to get their business off the ground.

Context: The biggest caveat to taking out loans is that you have to pay them back with interest. Ensure that you have a secure and reasonable plan to pay them back. It is highly recommended that you work with a professional financial advisor to build loan fees into your finances. Lastly, check your credit score. A good credit score is often required to take out loans.

If you are considering taking out loans, know what options are available to your specific business structure. For example, if you register as an L3C, you have the ability to go to a family foundation and be considered a non-profit to get a low interest loan or interest free loan. Check with your financial advisor about what options best suit your business structure.

Loans often have reporting requirements. Don't be afraid of these requirements, as they can be beneficial to help you organize your finances and perpetuate good, sustainable business practices.

Use the following resources to assess your personal credit score and find financial assistance:

- Annual Credit Report
- Credit Karma
- National Foundation of Credit Counseling
- Small Business Administration
- Small Business Development Center

Additional Platforms for Raising Loans:

- Lending Club
- Prosper
- Kiva
- Do your research to find local, regional or even national foundations that may have additional opportunities

Even if you don't plan on using loans to start your business, always be aware that there are multiple loans available to help maintain businesses, much in the same way the PPP loans aided many businesses during the height of Covid-19.

Additional Resources: For links to the resources provided on this page, *see Resources, Loans.*

Related Patterns: Financials - Business Structure, Financials - Community Partnerships

Sources of Additional and Higher Margin Income

Utility: Additional revenue streams are essential for Farm Stops to remain economically viable; they are a core component of this business model. The consignment model Farm Stops use is designed to reward small-scale producers and enhance their financial sustainability. Ultimately, this means that Farm Stops will need additional revenue than the 20-35 percent margin afforded through consignment. For reference, a typical retail markup is 50-60 percent to cover operational costs.

In my research, I did not find a Farm Stop that had not in some way diversified their revenue.

Context: Diversifying your revenue makes your business more profitable, which allows you to enhance your store's sustainability and community impact. It also allows you to make your space more vibrant, and to get creative in the many ways you can serve your community.

Many Farm Stops have incorporated the following as additional revenue generation:

- Café
- Incubator Kitchen
- Educational Classes
- Cooking Demonstrations
- Additional Outdoor Farmer's Markets
- Community Supported Agriculture (CSA) subscription services
- Online Store
- Wholesale Merchandise
- Tavern Licenses (selling Beer and Wine)
- Rentable Community Space

Included below are additional details on cafés, subscription services, educational classes and community events, incubator kitchens, and online stores; but feel free to research any of the other options listed, or to get creative with additional ideas.

Don't Spread Yourself Too Thin!

Additional income sources are a wonderful way to support your bottom line, but they do require additional resources and management. If you want to incorporate multiple avenues, approach them one at a time. For example, don't try to open your store alongside a commercial kitchen, incubator kitchen, rentable community space and café all at once unless you have the systems, resources, and people set in place. Most stores have opened with a commercial kitchen or on-site café, and added other income sources at a later time when they were ready and able.

Table 9: Consider the following when adding other income sources:

People	Ensure you have a reliable team of people to help manage each revenue stream. Make sure that this team is trained in the proper skill sets, including Food Safety and Standard Operating Procedures.
Budget	Create a separate budget for the resources necessary to make your revenue stream a success. The last thing any store owner wants is for their diversified revenue streams to take over and put their business in debt. Try to estimate how this additional source of income will support your bottom line. Use the sample spreadsheet in *Resources, Funding Mechanisms* to understand how to incorporate diversified revenue stream estimates into your bottom line. This will help you to get a better sense of the material and staffing costs of this aspect of your business, and will better help you manage different streams.
Space	Figure out the size of the space you would like to devote to additional income sources. This is particularly important when it comes to designing a café, a commercial or incubator kitchen, or rentable community space.

Remember that additional income sources should align with your mission!

Related Patterns: Financials - Funding Mechanisms, Getting Started - Mission, Operations - Payroll and Staffing, Financials - Community Partnerships, Operations - Optimizing Store Layout, Financials - Café, Financials - Subscription Services, Financials - Educational Classes and Community Events, Financials - Incubator Kitchens and Rentable Community Spaces, Financials - Online Store.

Café

Utility: A café is not only a great source of income for your store, but it also encourages customers to spend more time in your store, showcase additional local producers that specialize in coffee, tea, baked goods, breads and other ready-made products; and build community among customers and producers.

Context: There are many ways to design a café in your store. You can make it as large or as small as you like, just be sure that it fits within your budget.

However you choose to design your café, keep in mind that it is important to integrate it within your market, as its placement is incredibly important for generating sales and encouraging customers to spend time there. For example, Argus Farm Stop in Ann Arbor, MI placed their café at the entrance to the store, with the grocery section set off to the side so that customers are drawn into the café to grab a drink or snack, and then are led into the grocery section to complete their purchases.

Consider the following when developing a café:

- Hire additional staff
- Train these staff with the appropriate skill sets
- Invest in certain equipment (ex. espresso machine)
- Ensure you procure the proper County, City, or State Regulatory Licensing and ensure accordance with Building Codes (See *Operations - Licensing*)

- Designate specific space for seating
- Align the hours of your café with the hours of your market.
- Use the café as an additional space to showcase local artisanal crafts, gifts and snacks

Related Patterns: Financials - Funding Mechanisms, Operations - Licensing, Operations - Payroll and Staffing, Financials - Wholesale Options, Communication - Producer Relationships, Financials - Community Partnerships, Operations - Optimizing Store Layout

Incubator Kitchens and Rentable Community Spaces

Utility: Some existing Farm Stops offer rentable community spaces or an incubator kitchen. These areas can be rented by community members, or local businesses who don't have production spaces of their own. Thus, these spaces diversify your income, and allow community members and other local businesses to further engage with and take advantage of your store.

Before opening an incubator kitchen or rentable community space, it's important to do your research! Talk to as many people or similar organizations that operate these spaces as possible. Explore the availability of shared work and community spaces in your area.

Context: If you plan on establishing a commercial kitchen in your store, you may also consider offering a small portion of that space, or the entire space on specific days, to other local food producers who may not have access to commercial production spaces.

Incubator kitchens can also offer small-business owners additional services like business development training and access to packaging and label printing. They also offer a space for small-businesses to distribute their products.

For example, Local Roots in Wooster, OH offers local bakers and value-added producers access to a commercially licensed kitchen for a small rental fee. Typically these businesses would not be able to afford developing their own commercial kitchens. As a result, their store features these producers' creations, and the producers benefit from having a production and distribution space.

Community spaces don't have to be limited just to the kitchen, however. Random Harvest in Craryville, NY offers certified local health practitioners a small room for massage, light, sound, and yoga therapies if they are unable to operate out of their own space. They also offer a rentable community events space for private parties to host dinners, celebrations, and other classes for a small fee. Community events spaces are a great way to expand the scope of how your store can serve your community.

Keep in mind, however, that this option also requires separate staff to manage operations and logistics. There are often many moving parts to managing an incubator kitchen, or offering community and event spaces. You'll be thankful for the extra hands to manage them.

Related Patterns: Location - Physical Space, Operations - Payroll and Staffing, Operations - Optimizing Store Layout, Operations - Licensing

Subscription Services

Utility: Adding a subscription service for various local goods in your store not only helps to further engage customers, but is also a great way to showcase the producers you work with and to provide them with additional income.

Context: Subscription services are modeled after traditional Community Supported Agriculture programs in which customers sign up to receive a box of fresh produce curated by the staff at your store. These boxes can be distributed on a weekly, biweekly, monthly or ongoing basis, but whichever you choose, make sure this remains consistent for your customers.

You can then decide which days to offer pick-up, whether you would like to offer delivery as an option, and whether you would like to offer add-ons such as bread, flowers, eggs, meat, value-added items or additional produce. If you offer delivery, consider implementing an additional fee if necessary.

Starting a subscription service is essentially starting an entirely new wing of your business. Make sure you are prepared for the level of coordination and effort it takes to make these programs run smoothly and successfully!

Table 10: Key things to know when starting a subscription service

Staffing	Sourcing and Storage	Timing
You need to hire additional staff. Remember that this is an entirely separate aspect of your operation that requires its own inventory management system, and coordination of many logistics. You'll be thankful for hiring individuals to manage it!	You need to be able to source and store enough product to maintain quantities throughout the duration of the program. This can be challenging during certain seasons when there may be fewer produce offerings.	Timing is everything! Make sure your core business is stable before developing a subscription service, and that it won't take away from other operational activities. It is not recommended you attempt a subscription service unless you have the resources and staff already in place.

Additional Things to Consider when Curating a Subscription Service:
- Price of your subscription.
- Size of your membership.
- Length of subscription:
  - Options may include: Seasonal weekly, biweekly or monthly boxes (ex. May-October); or ongoing, year-long subscriptions (made available weekly, biweekly, or monthly).
  - Keep your location in mind as some areas may not be able to sustain year-round subscriptions.
- Customer Relations:
  - Requests to switch pick-up days/times to accommodate life events such as vacations.
  - Frequently asked questions and concerns.
  - Preferences and dietary restrictions.
- Online platforms such as those outlined below can help organize many of these details.
  - Whichever platform you choose, make sure that it is able to integrate with your existing Point of Sale system.

Examples of Subscription Services:

Argus Farm Stop in Ann Arbor, MI curates a weekly offering of produce they call the Weekly Produce Box. The subscription includes 7-10 produce items. Members pick up their produce on Thursdays at one of their three locations. The box is offered year-round.

Local Roots in Wooster, OH curates a seasonal weekly subscription service for the summer and winter. Their summer boxes focus primarily on summer produce, while their winter boxes focus primarily on value-added items, prepared foods, meat, and winter vegetables.

To aid in managing inventory, consider using one of the following online platforms:

- **Shopify**
- **Squarespace**
- **Local Line**
- **Barn2Door**
- **Harvie**

- **Farmigo**
- **Mercato**
- **Local Food Marketplace**
- **Square**

Be sure to research any additional online selling platforms that may be out there, and to speak with other stores or organizations that currently offer subscription programs.

Additional Resources: For links to the resources provided on this page, see *Resources, Sources of Additional and Higher Margin Income - Subscription Services.*

Related Patterns: Operations - Payroll and Staffing, Operations - Optimizing Store Layout, Location - Storage, Operations - Point of Sale, Operations - Online Store.

Educational Classes and Community Events

Utility: Your community is critical to the success of your business. It provides the shoppers, the energy, and the relationships that will enhance the cultural value of your business. Many stores take advantage of the myriad skills and resources their producers can offer to curate classes and events on a number of topics from cheese and salsa making, to medicinal herb demonstrations, to yoga classes and crafting sessions.

Additionally, stores can also organize community events that feature other local businesses or artists such as outdoor concerts with local musicians, food-truck festivals, and art fairs.

Context: Educational classes and community events are a useful way to engage your community, make use of existing or new partnerships with other local businesses, and further showcase your producers. They also allow you to express your creativity and align your store's mission with particular activities, events or organizations.

Just be sure that whatever events and classes you choose to hold align with your mission.

5 Tips for Organizing Educational Classes or Community Events:

1. **Identify an Events Coordinator within your organization.**
   a. Use tools and resources, such as **Eventbrite** or **Brown Paper Tickets** to help plan and market events.
   b. Determine your space and staffing capacity to host events.
   c. Consider adding an events calendar to your website, or in your store.
2. **Plan as far in advance as you can.**
   a. Helps with having enough time to gather important materials
   b. Ensures you have ample time to advertise the event(s) to your community
3. **Maintain Community Partnerships.**
   a. You never know when inspiration will strike and you will want to partner with a local jewelry or candle maker, forager or herbalist, chef, or beer or wine-maker.
   b. Local networks, such as **NextDoor**, are a useful way to connect with your community.
   c. You can also use online resources, such as **Zoom**, to facilitate events.
4. **Be creative!**
   a. The possibilities are endless when it comes to finding ways to engage your customers. Don't be afraid to think outside the box and consider ideas that have not yet been done!
   b. Remember: mission-oriented events should take priority.
5. **Make the events as accessible and as interactive as possible.**

Related Patterns: Financials - Community Partnerships, Financials - Community Events as Fundraisers, Operations - Payroll and Staffing, Operations - Optimizing Store Layout, Communication - Marketing

Online Store

Utility: In this digital age, most small businesses have some, if not all, of their products available online. Developing an online store can diversify your revenue, expand your offerings, increase the accessibility of your store (particularly if you offer delivery), ensure a level of resiliency in the face of supply chain shortages, and also provide additional sales outlets for your producers.

Context: These days, an online store can easily be embedded into your existing website. For example, if your website is designed by SquareSpace, you can easily embed a SquareSpace e-commerce store into your existing website. You can also choose to use a separate online platform in addition to your existing website.

Table 11: Online platforms for food retail establishments, local farms and small-businesses

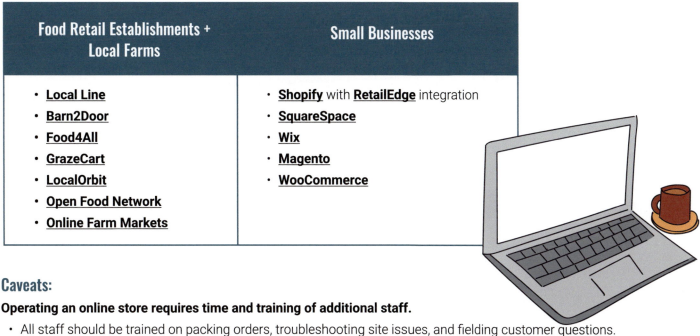

Food Retail Establishments + Local Farms	Small Businesses
• **Local Line** • **Barn2Door** • **Food4All** • **GrazeCart** • **LocalOrbit** • **Open Food Network** • **Online Farm Markets**	• **Shopify** with **RetailEdge** integration • **SquareSpace** • **Wix** • **Magento** • **WooCommerce**

Caveats:

Operating an online store requires time and training of additional staff.
- All staff should be trained on packing orders, troubleshooting site issues, and fielding customer questions.
- Conversely, make sure you always have at least one staff member on shift who understands how to operate and troubleshoot the online store.
- Always have on hand a number staff can call to help with troubleshooting issues.

Physical Space
- Whatever space you think you have for packing online orders? Double it.

Additional Resources: For links to the resources provided on this page, see *Resources, Sources of Additional and Higher Margin Income - Online Store.*

Related Patterns: Communication - Marketing, Location - Physical Space, Operations - Payroll and Staffing, Operations - Point of Sale, Financials - Funding Mechanisms.

Table 12: Consider the following when looking to build an online store:

Cost

Third-party platforms often require a monthly or yearly subscription.

Search Engine Optimization (SEO)

This helps customize your name and URL so people can better find your website.

Scalability

Choose a platform that will allow for growth!

Simple and Mobile-Friendly User Interface

Ensure the site is easily accessible via phones and tablets, and easy to navigate.

Site Speed

No one likes long loading times or websites that freeze. Make sure your site can accommodate many requests.

Software Integration with Point of Sale

You may need to connect third-party applications, specifically as they apply to your Point of Sale system, to enable online purchases and other features.

This will also help you to manage inventory, which can also become further complicated through e-commerce. Use programs such as RetailEdge to integrate into your Point of Sale system inventory monitoring.

Staffing Needs

Make sure you have enough staff to support packing and delivering orders, fielding customer questions and managing inventory.

Physical Space

Packing orders requires space. Especially if you prioritize store pick-up. Designate a space in your store where your staff can quickly and efficiently pack orders.

Marketing

Make sure your customers know you have an online store, and how to access it. Use your social media channels, and inform customers of the new online option.

Social Programs: SNAP/EBT

Utility: SNAP is a federal nutrition assistance program to help make food more accessible to individuals and families of lower socioeconomic status who qualify for food stamps. SNAP stands for Supplemental Nutrition Assistance Program, and makes use of an Electronic Benefits Transfer (EBT) card. This card is used like a debit card to allow individuals and families of lower socioeconomic status to purchase food in authorized retail food stores.

Context: Getting SNAP/EBT authorization enhances your store's accessibility and inclusivity, and ensures that a wider population is able to receive the same fresh, healthy produce and products you carry. SNAP/EBT enhances your store's value to, and support for, your community.

Applying to be an authorized retail food store may seem daunting, but don't be discouraged!

The **USDA Food and Nutrition Service** clearly defines the process on their website and provides a number you may call with additional questions or concerns: 1-877-823-4369.

In addition to the application itself, you must also complete the **Retailer Training Materials** offered by the USDA Food and Nutrition Service. This ensures that you understand the rules and regulations of being a SNAP/EBT authorized retail food store. These trainings also provide knowledge about which foods are eligible, SNAP sales tax, manufacturer's coupons, and your point of sale equipment. It is important to note that your point of sale system must be compatible with SNAP/EBT authorization. Finally, these training materials provide you with the proper USDA authorized signage to advertise that you accept SNAP/EBT benefits.

Please note that offering online SNAP/EBT benefits varies by state and requires a different application process. See *Resources - Social Programs: SNAP/EBT for additional information.*

Lastly, ensure that your staff are well-trained in any record-keeping requirements, and in flagging eligible in-store and online inventory. It is importnat to make sure your customers know which products they may purchase via SNAP/EBT benefits.

Additional Programming

Many states have created additions to SNAP/EBT benefits. Below are two examples of additional programming that currently exists in multiple states.

Double-Up Food Bucks:
- The **Fair Food Fund** created **Double-Up Food Bucks (DUFB)** which allows individuals and families to double their SNAP benefits when they buy fresh, locally grown items. DUFB is now available in 25 states. See Resources - Social Programs: SNAP/EBT to learn more about how to engage with DUFB.

SNAP Stretch:
- The Wild Ramp in Huntington, West Virginia (WV) has created a program called **SNAP Stretch** in conjunction with the WV Food & Farm Coalition, WVU Extension SNAP Education, the WV Farmers' Market Association, and the USDA FINI Program. See Resources - Social Programs: SNAP/EBT to learn more about SNAP Stretch. Be sure to explore the different offerings in your state!

Once you have completed your application and the training materials, ensure that your community knows that you offer SNAP/EBT benefits. This can be done using the appropriate signage provided by the USDA in the windows of your store, as well as with social media campaigns, email newsletters, and on your website. Marketing SNAP/EBT benefits is a wonderful opportunity to expand your customer base and influence, as it often provides additional opportunities to work with community centers and school groups.

Additional Resources: For links to the resources provided on this page, see *Resources, Social Programs: SNAP/EBT.*

Related Patterns: Operations - Point of Sale, Operations - Licensing, Operations - Payroll and Staffing, Communication - Marketing

LOCATION

Location

Overview: As the famous real estate mantra goes, "It's all about location, location, location!" Where you decide to put your store in your community determines the visibility and accessibility for both consumers and also producers. Heightened visibility ensures that your store is able to interact with your community in a number of different ways, and enhanced accessibility determines how easily producers and consumers can access your store.

Context: When considering location, understand your community's demographics. This can help you to prioritize a location that falls on a high foot-traffic area, a high-car traffic area, or whether it's best that your location has access to public transportation. Understanding the demographics of your area can also help you know the size of your ideal location. Remember, the goal is to ensure your store is as accessible to your community as possible.

Table of Contents:

Key Tips to Help You Source Your Location:

Use your networks.

Seek out others in your community who may have tips on finding a location. For example, ask the city or county office, local universities, or other small-business owners how they were able to secure their location.

Locate high foot-traffic areas.

Try to locate an area that has high foot-traffic, often located near other shops, restaurants and community spaces. This may otherwise be known as the main drag of the community.

Many stores, such as Argus Farm Stop, in Ann Arbor, MI; Local Roots in Wooster, OH; The Wild Ramp in Huntington, WV; and Boone Street Market in Jonesborough TN, benefit greatly from a high-foot traffic location.

The Small Business Development Center in your area can provide demographic and traffic data to help you gain a better understanding of how your business would function in your community.

Locate high car-traffic streets.

If your community doesn't have a high foot-traffic area, you may want to look at the busiest high car-traffic areas. Large signs, outdoor displays, and available parking can all attract drivers to stop and shop.

Provide ample parking.

See *Parking*.

Be mindful of proximity to public transportation.

Even if your store is located in a walkable or heavily trafficked area, many in your community, both customers and employees alike, may rely solely on public transportation to get around. Some cities may also offer discounted bus passes, which enhances the accessibiity of your store if located near bus stops.

Make sure the location is a place you want to be in!

Even if you are looking at an abandoned building for your location, assess how you feel in that space, and whether you can envision yourself and others working and shopping there.

Potential Challenges: An ideal location would likely have all of these elements. But of course, the perfect location does not always exist, and if it does, it may not be available. Sometimes, you have to prioritize which of the above aspects are most important to you. For example, choosing a high foot-traffic area may mean you have less space for parking, or producer drop off. Conversely, having a high car-traffic location may mean you have fewer walk-in customers, but you may have more space for producer drop-off and customer parking.

Related Patterns: Location - Parking, Operations - Physical Space, Financials - Community Partnerships, Communication - Community Demographics.

Parking

Utility: Parking is an important aspect of determining whether your location is right for your business. While it's not always essential, it can enhance the accessibility of your store for customers, and also ensure producers have adequate space to drop off their goods.

Context: Parking often depends on the location of your building, and the use of nearby spots and lots. In urban and semi-urban areas, it is worth noting that parking can be a rare commodity, especially if your store is located along a busy main street or highway.

Table 13: Examples of Farm Stop Parking Arrangements

Random Harvest, NY	Because their store is located along a scenic highway, and is located in an old Victorian house, they were able to include a parking lot next to the building that allows cars to efficiently pull in.
Argus Farm Stop, MI	Argus has three locations within an urban area. One of their locations has three spaces in the front of the store. These spaces are often used for producer drop-off as well, so they also make use of side-street parking. The other location has 10 spots, but also makes use of side-street parking. Argus was also able to work directly with the city council to convert previously marked, "no-parking" areas to 30 minute parking spots. Consider strengthening that relationship with your city council!
Local Roots, OH and The Wild Ramp, WV	While both stores are located along a busy stretch of their communities, they are able to make use of large parking lots in the back of their buildings, as well as street parking along the front and sides.
Acorn Farmers Market and Café, MI	Has seven spaces in front of the store, and 14 across the street with several parking lots within walking distance.

Other Considerations:

- **Communicate parking alternatives with your customers:**
  - If you do not yet have access to a parking lot, clearly communicate to your customers either on your website or your storefront where the nearest available parking is.
- **Encourage non-parking alternatives:**
  - If parking around your store is limited, or if you don't like the look of a large lot by your store, put out a bike rack and encourage customers to bike or walk instead if this is feasible for your location.
- **Producer drop-off:**
  - Don't exclude the needs of your producers! If you do have parking available, set aside a portion of that space as a loading dock. This enhances convenience for producers, and helps you organize your inventory system as you can more easily monitor what was dropped off, by who and when.
  - It is highly recommended that you hire a manager to oversee producer drop-off. See *Payroll and Staffing* for additional information about specific roles.
  - Be mindful and respectful of, and transparent with, your neighbors when designating producer drop-off zones. This may increase traffic and noise, which may upset some neighbors.
  - If your store is located in a primarily high foot-traffic area, you may not need as many parking spots. If this is the case, use any extra spots for producer drop off.
- **Develop a relationship with the governing body of your community:**
  - They may be able to reserve street parking, help you purchase a nearby lot, or even convert nearby "no-parking" spaces for your store.
  - Keep in mind that purchasing or building a lot, reserving street parking, or altering existing parking structures may require the city's or county's approval. Get creative and communicate with your city council members to change parking around your store to best fit your needs and help you create a vibrant business.

Related Patterns: Location, Location - Physical Space, Location - Community Demographics, Financials - Community Partnerships, Operations - Optimizing Store Layout, Operations - Licensing, Operations - Payroll and Staffing

Physical Space

Utility: The physical space of your store often determines the atmosphere, and shapes your customers' shopping experiences. It also determines whether customers are able to find what they need, and if producers are able to navigate the space quickly and efficiently. Lastly, it determines how much room you have for office space, storage, and a break area for your staff.

Office space and employee break areas are incredibly important. Do not forget to include these aspects in your layout. Your office space should be big enough to hold a desk or two, book shelves, filing cabinets, and a printer as well as typical office supplies. You may also want to invest in a label-maker and a laminator for creating labels for products in the store. See *Optimizing Store Layout - Display* for more information on generating labels.

Your staff break area should have ample seating, and should be located in an area where staff feel they can rest, relax and take a break.

Consider the following when designing your store, or searching for a location:

Mobility

Utility: Ensure that your store is accessible to all persons of all abilities.

Context: Ensure that the exterior and interior structure of your store is compliant with **The Americans with Disabilities Act Small Business Guidelines.** This certification typically aligns with your city ordinance building codes, and often requires installing certain elements such as:

- Aisles that are wide enough to accommodate wheelchairs.
- Ramps at entrances both in and outside of the store as needed.
- Adjusting the height of counters or shelving to ensure people with disabilities may reach the items.

Local architecture and contracting companies may be able to assist you in fulfilling these guidelines. Be sure to check the **ADA Business Connection Guidebook.** See *Resources Physical Space - Mobility* for links to these resources.

Use your networks! It's always a good idea to reach out to other local businesses or individuals you know who have completed a construction project in your area. They can offer many recommendations and guidance on the process.

Additional Resources: For links to the resources provided on this page, see *Resources, Physical Space.*

Related Patterns: Operations - Optimizing Store Layout, Financials - Community Partnerships, Location - Community Demographics

46

Storage

Utility: Storage space is crucial for Farm Stops as it not only determines the amount of products you are able to carry at a given time, but it also determines how you manage your inventory.

Context: Look for locations that are either equipped to handle, or have the capacity to accommodate, multiple methods of storage throughout the store for:
- Dry and frozen goods on the selling floor:
  - Refrigerated units and coolers to hold frozen fruits, vegetables, soups, dairy products, meat and to-go meals, if offered.
  - Shelf space for dry goods (ex. Garlic, onions, potatoes, grains, oils, breads, etc.)
- Backstock of produce, meat, dairy and dry goods off the selling floor.
- Produce racks, boxes and packaging producers use to transfer their goods.
- Display materials such as signage, markers, shelving units, and tables.
- Returnable packaging materials such as milk and egg cartons, or berry containers.

Be mindful of how you store different types of products. See *Optimizing Store Layout - Display.*

Lastly, be sure to communicate effectively with your producers about the availability of storage, and how this may change throughout the year depending on the seasonality of products.

Here's an example of how to effectively use storage space in your store:

The Wild Ramp in Huntington, WV currently has 140 producers and operates in a space with a total of 2600 square feet.
- On the selling floor they have:
  - 4 merchandising coolers
  - 1 ice cream freezer
- For backstock they have:
  - 2 walk-in refrigerators
  - 2 back-stock freezers for meat products
  - 2 additional backstock freezers and 2 backstock refrigerators for their attached commercial kitchen.
  - They recently received a grant to put in 5 additional merchandising coolers outside their selling floor to accommodate frozen to-go meals made in their commercial kitchen.

Related Patterns: Operations - Optimizing Store Layout, Operations - Payroll and Staffing, Communication - Producer Relationships, Operations - Types of Goods

Table 14: Things to Keep in Mind about Storage

Increased Costs

The more storage space you add in the form of refrigerators and freezers, the higher your electricity bill.

More refrigerators and freezers also increases the need for maintenance, which can also result in additional costs.

Key Tips: Put your backstock refrigerators and freezers on the outside of the building. That way, you're not spending as much money heating up the inside to accommodate for the temperature change.

Increased Maintenance

More freezers and refrigerators also require more maintenance and staff training in the event a problem occurs.

Take some time to train your staff on how to track trends in temperature fluctuations in your refrigeration system. This can help to alert you to any potential problems that might otherwise be disastrous.

For example: Random Harvest in Craryville, NY had a freezer outage during one summer that resulted in pounds of ice cream wasted, which is sad not only for the consumers who love ice cream, but also for the producers who lost their product. Don't let this happen to you!

Key Tips:

- Have a handyperson on staff, or have someone you trust in your community on call to handle emergencies.
- If an outage occurs, you will have to reimburse the producers working on the consignment model as you were the caretaker for their lost product.
- Know which other local businesses also have freezer or refrigerator space, and develop an agreement to help each other in case of emergencies.
- Install a generator if you have the resources available.

Noise and Heat

Refrigerators and freezers are noisy. This may interrupt customers' experience, or any potential classes or events you may host inside the store.

Key Tips:

- If you have the funds available, try putting some soundboards along the ceiling to reduce noise.
- Consider consulting with an architect to put the refrigerator compressors outside the building to reduce noise and excess heat.

Optimizing Your Space

Typically, refrigeration must reside along an external wall. This is often a foundational piece when organizing your space.

Key Tips: See *Optimizing Store Layout* to learn about organizational practices to enhance your customers' experience.

Security

Ensure that these storage areas are locked and secured, and that only your staff has access to these areas.

Key Tips: Leave the keys or combinations to all refrigerators and coolers in a secure, yet known, location to your staff.

Community Spaces

Utility: Offering community spaces creates a place for people to come together, share experiences, and enrich the culture of your community, thereby enhancing the value of your store for the people you serve. Even if the events you host are free to the public, offering community spaces is another great way to further diversify your revenue as it draws more people into your store.

Think about all the times you may have had some work to do, or a good book to read, or wanted to meet a friend somewhere. Offering community spaces allows people to do just that, and so much more, and are often known as Third Places. Third Places are defined as places where people can simply hang out, enjoy each other's company, or learn together through curated classes and events.

Context: There are many different ways to creatively implement community spaces in your store, aside from creating a café. For example:

- Set aside an area of your store for customer seating where people can enjoy some of the goods they just purchased.
- Set aside a certain portion of space either inside or outside to host events and classes.
- Designate certain rooms or areas that people may rent out for private events.
- Create a rentable space to offer other local businesses such as healing, art, music or nutrition-related services (See *Incubator Kitchens and Rentable Community Spaces*)

Consider the following when developing a Community Space:
- Determine any necessary materials such as seating, lighting and other decorations.
- The atmosphere. You may want to let your employees take turns curating playlists to play over speakers, or to get creative in decorating the space.
- Cleanliness. Keep the space clean and tidy.
- Ensure all staff are trained in the maintenance of the space.

How Stores Have Incorporated Community Spaces:

Random Harvest, NY
- They use their outdoor space to host community events such as music showcases, arts and crafts fairs, and farm-to-table dinners.
- They rent a space on the second floor of their building as a place for people to host private events, classes or dinners.
- They also designated a separate room on the second floor of their building as a "Healing Room" for wellness and health practitioners to offer their services to the community. This room runs on a 75/25 percent consignment ratio for practitioners who wish to rent it.
- Lastly, they offer a café with ample seating for customers to enjoy meals made in-house through their commercial kitchen.

Local Roots, OH
- They feature a wonderful café with ample seating facing the grocery section of the store, as well as an artisan and crafts section where customers can enjoy purchasing gifts or housewares for themselves or loved ones.
- They have also paired up with local food trucks to host out-door seasonal celebrations and festivities.

Argus Farm Stop, MI
- They feature a greenhouse structure attached to their Liberty Street location where they host ticketed and free events and classes that showcase music, arts and other food-related ventures in their community.
- When not used for events and classes, this greenhouse holds ample indoor and outdoor seating for customers to enjoy to-go meals prepared by a local restaurant, or a drink made in their café.

Source: Argus Farm Stop. (n.d). Liberty Street Greenhouse.

Picture 1: Argus Farm Stop's greenhouse at their Liberty Street location. This is a community space where customers can gather with friends to share a snack or drink. It is also used as an events space, and a place to showcase local artists.

Source: Argus Farm Stop. (n.d). Liberty Street Greenhou

Picture 2: The Wild Ramp uses their outdoor space to curate community events such as annual farm-to-table dinners.

Source: Argus Farm Stop. (n.d). Packard Street Community Space.

Picture 3: Argus Farm Stop also has a separate location with indoor seating that is often used for community events, such as craft beer tastings.

Source: Lawrence Braun (n.d). Random Harvest Market.

Picture 4: Random Harvest has a beautiful café that offers customers and community members a place to engage with each other over fresh, in-house made meals with locally sourced ingredients.

Related Patterns: Financials - Incubator Kitchens and Rentable Community Spaces, Financials - Community Partnerships, Financials - Community Events as Fundraisers, Operations - Optimizing Your Layout, Financials - Sources of Additional and Higher Margin Income

Size of Sellable Space

Utility: Knowing the size of the sellable space in your store is important for determining how much product you can display, as well as how much product you can store both on and off the selling floor. This directly determines how many different products you can display at the same time, and influences the overall layout of your store. Keep in mind that the size of sellable space in your store will be measured in square footage.

Context: Farm stops exist and operate on a number of different scales ranging from 800–5,000 square feet of sellable space that accommodates anywhere from 70 to over 200 producers at a time. This variability speaks to the fact that it's not always the size of the space, but how you arrange it that makes all the difference. With that variability in mind, aim to find a space larger than 800 square feet, as anything less begins to limit mobility, accessibility, and your capacity to work with multiple producers.

Most food retailers place refrigerators and freezers on the outer walls, and then fill the remaining space in the center with dried goods, and non-refrigerated products. This not only helps to anchor your layout, but it also creates a natural flow to your store. *See Operations - Optimizing Store Layout* for more ideas on how to get creative and make the most of your sellable space.

Lastly, estimate how many producers you anticipate working with, and how much storage space you may need to accommodate their products. This will help you find or build your location.

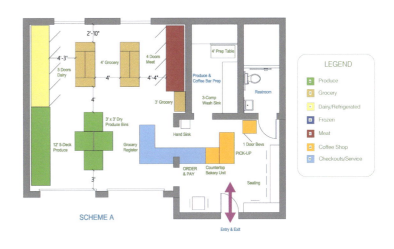

Figure 3: A sample of Argus Farm Stop's floor layout.

Size of Sellable Space

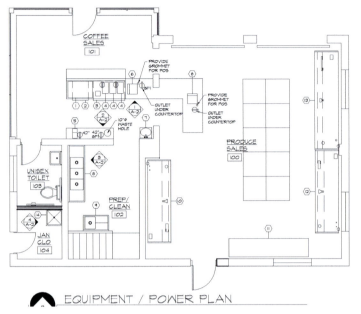

EQUIPMENT / POWER PLAN

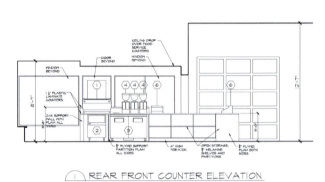

REAR FRONT COUNTER ELEVATION

EQUIPMENT SCHEDULE

#	ITEM	MFR & MODEL #	QUANTITY	SIZE (LxDxH)*	FURNISHED BY	INSTALLED BY	ELECTRICAL	GAS	PLUMBING	DRAIN	NOTES
1	Espresso Machine	La Marzocco GB/5	1	37.5" x 24.5" x 19"	Owner	Contractor	220V / 60HZ / 1PH / 40A	-	1/2" CW	Air gap	-
2	Ice Machine	Scotsman CU1526MA-1A	1	26" x 27" x 33"	Owner	Contractor	115V / 60HZ / 1PH / 15A	-	3/4" CW	Air gap	Air-cooled
3	Counter height refrigeration	TRUE (TUC-48-ADA)	1	48.4" x 30.3" x 29.8"	Owner	Contractor	115V/ 60HZ/1PH/5.0A	-	-	-	-
4	Grinder	Mazzer - KONY	3	9.5" x 16.5" x 25.5"	Owner	Owner	115V/ 60HZ/1PH	-	-	-	-
5	Cash Register	--	2	--	Owner	Owner	115V / 60HZ / 1PH	-	-	-	-
6	Hot Water Dispenser	Bunn HW2	1	7" x 14.3" x 23.8"	Owner	Contractor	120V/1 PH/60HZ/15A	-	1/4" CW	-	-
7	Hand Sink, Wall	Eagle HSA-10	1	15" x 19" x 7.5"	Contractor	Contractor	--	-	1/2" H&CW	Direct	w/ soap & towel dispensers
8	3-compartment sink	Advance Tabco 93-3-54-18RL	1	27.5" x 84" x 37.5"	Owner	Contractor	--	-	1/2" H&CW	Air gap	Provide drip-shelf as shown
9	1-compartment sink	Advance Tabco 93-1-24-18R	1	40" x 27" x 37"	Owner	Contractor	--	-	1/2" H&CW	Air gap	-
10	High Merchandiser	Hillphoenix ONRBH	1	10' x 35" x 87"	Owner	Contractor	120V/ 60HZ / 1PH, 1.17 A**	-	-	Air gap	-
11	Display Shelves		1	10' x 16" x 87"	Owner	Contractor	-	-	-	-	-
12	Reach-in Merchandiser	Hillphoenix ORZH	1	10' x 42" x 87"	Owner	Contractor	120V/ 60HZ / 1PH, 3.2 A**	-	-	Air gap	-
13	High Merchandiser	Hillphoenix ON5DMH	1	12' x 36" x 87"	Owner	Contractor	120V/ 60HZ / 1PH, 1.17 A**	-	-	Air gap	-
14	Service Sink		1	24" x 24"	Contractor	Contractor	--	-	1/2" H&CW	Direct	w/ mop hanger

The above are two sample schematics from Argus Farm Stop that show how they were able to optimize their sellable space to include a café within their grocery section.

The Equipment Schedule is a legend for both schematic diagrams.: the equipment number in the leftmost column corresponds with the numbers on the schematics. This legend also provides model, quantity, size, plumbing and electrical information for most of the specified equipment to give you a better sense of what to look for when building out your space.

Related Patterns: Operations - Optimizing Store Layout, Operations - Types of Goods

Community Demographics

Utility: Understanding your community's demographics helps you assess how your store's mission may serve your community's specific needs, as well as how your store can further engage with your community. Most existing Farm Stops began as a way to connect communities with local farmers and producers, and to grow the local food economy to benefit the community.

For example, Acorn Farmer's Market and Café in Manchester, MI was developed because they lost the only grocery store in their community. Local Roots in Wooster, OH was developed because the founder noticed a demand in the community for a centralized location for people to purchase local food. Thus, your community's needs will influence the overall growth and development of your store.

More than that, understanding demographic information can inform the visibility of your store, as well as certain elements of your business plan such as: the best ways to market your store to the community; what your anticipated sales rate may be within the first few years of operation based on the average income of your area; what specialized services you want to prioritize; and, what your parking and accessibility needs are.

Context: Consider the following ways demographic information can help develop your store:

- Is there a higher population of older residents in the community?
  - This informs whether you locate your store near reliable public transportation routes, or offer more flexible parking options.
- Is there a considerable population in need of food assistance or other social programs?
  - This informs how your store prioritizes offering social programs like SNAP/EBT and Double Up Food Bucks.
- Does your community lack community spaces or gathering places?
  - This informs how often you hold events and classes, what types of events and classes you offer, and whether you want to prioritize creating a Community Space such as a café.

The US Census Bureau offers a very useful **QuickFacts Tool** that helps you understand the overall makeup of your community. They also offer a useful tool, called the **Census Business Builder**, to help people develop their business plan around specific community demographics.

Other useful resources to obtain and analyze demographic data include:
- Your local **Small Business Development Center**
- **DataUSA**
- **TownCharts**
- **The American Library Association**

Related Patterns: Getting Started - Mission, Financials- Social Programs: SNAP/EBT, Location, Financials - Sources of Additional and Higher Margin Income, Communication - Marketing, Location - Parking, Location - Community Spaces, Financials - Community Partnerships

COMMUNICATION

Communication

Overview: Communication is more than just knowing how to market your business, it's about the relationships you generate within your community. This chapter not only provides information on various marketing methods and strategies to send the right message to your community about who you are, and what you offer; but it also expands on the importance of developing key partnerships with other local businesses, town or city governing entities, and community members. More than that, this section emphasizes fostering and maintaining relationships with the most invaluable people in your community: your producers! Remember that these individuals will be your greatest advocates, and will truly help to make your store a success, no matter the amount of social media you send out (though that helps too).

Table of Contents:

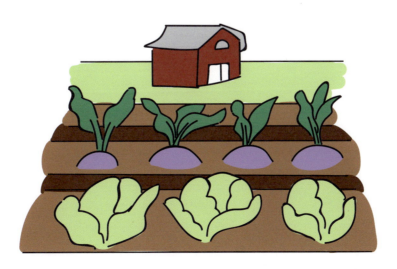

Marketing

Utility: Of course, marketing is a critical aspect for any small business just getting their feet off the ground. In our current day and age, there are many ways you can market your business.

Context: While most existing Farm Stops have had success with word-of-mouth advertising, there are many other ways to market your business in your community.

Before you begin to market yourself, there are two things you must consider:
- **Create an online presence**. An online presence is crucial for establishing a credible business. This can take the form of a website, a Google Business page, a listing on related sites, or on social media. These mechanisms help those interested in your business to learn about who you are and what you do.
- **Prioritize your Producer Relationships.** These relationships are one of the most important methods of word-of-mouth advertising. Producers who support your mission and enjoy working with you will inevitably tell others of your store, including additional prospective producers as well as customers from their other sales outlets. See *Producer Relationships* to understand how to foster and maintain these relationships.

Below are some suggestions on how to market your business virtually, and with more traditional methods. Please note that some of the suggested services may have monthly charges that you may need to work into your budget.

Virtual Marketing Methods

Below are some suggestions on how to market your business virtually, and with more traditional methods. Please note that some of the suggested services may have monthly charges that you may need to work into your budget.

A well-designed website: This is a crucial tool that provides a coherent space for anyone interested in your business's mission and services. It can also help members of your community directly connect with you should you choose to include contact information, or a way to sign up for e-newsletters.
- It is highly recommended that you find an experienced web designer to professionally set up your website. This is worth the investment.
- See *Online Store* for suggestions on some available web platforms. Some platforms can also provide you with analytics that help you understand how your store is interacting with your community.

Third-party advertisers: <u>Google Business</u> is wonderful for marketing your business as it enables others to leave reviews, and provides analytics to track your engagement.

Social media presence: Whether you use it regularly or not, social media is one of the most prevalent ways to market your business, specifically via popular platforms such as Facebook, Instagram, Twitter and TikTok.

- Consider assigning an individual or team devoted to developing and expanding your social media presence as what you post, how often you post, and when you post all matter towards engaging your community.
  - Make sure this person or team generates content that aligns with the image and messaging of your Mission.
- These platforms also provide businesses with analytics that measure how well your posts are received, and how others engage with your business. For example, **Facebook Business Suite** allows you to boost your posts, and offers advanced metrics on how to better engage your target audience.
- Take a moment to consider who your target audience may be before setting up your profiles, or sending out any posts.
  - See *Community Demographics* to understand how learning about your community can aid in determining your target audience.
- If you would rather not use platforms such as Facebook or Instagram, there are other social media platforms that are specifically designed to engage communities, such as **Nextdoor**.

Other Virtual Marketing Methods:

- **E-newsletters**
  - Have a link to sign up on your website and social media, if using.
  - Use third-party websites such as **Constant Contact** and **Mailchimp.**
- **Local periodicals**
  - Local magazines and newspapers can post a virtual ad or mention your business in their own e-newsletters, websites and social media. For example, Argus Farm Stop has a relationship with a local newspaper, The Observer.
  - See *Community Partnerships* for details on how to facilitate these connections.
- **List your business on other related sites such as:**
  - **Eat Well Guide**
  - **Farmers Market Coalition Directory**
  - **LocalHarvest**
    - You may want to monitor your listing here. They may remove it if someone thinks you're not a farmer's market.
    - This is also a good place to list events.
  - **Edible Communities**
- **Your local Chamber of Commerce and Visitors Bureau.**
  - Towns and cities are always looking to drum up opportunities for tourism. Listing your business on these sites can help entice others to visit your community and gain an interest in what you do. For example, Argus Farm Stop is listed via **Destination Ann Arbor**.
- **Use your local Small Business Development Center.** They can help you list your website on other pertinent related sites, and can help enhance Search Engine Optimization (SEO) so that your store quickly appears when searched online.

Traditional Marketing Methods

- **Word of Mouth:**
  - This method is your best friend! It costs nothing, and only requires you to be true to your mission and community. Try to target those most active in your community, as they are the ones most likely to spread the news.
  - This method depends on your store's location, and how visible it is to passersby.
- **Local Ads:**
  - Local ads in the form of fliers or posters placed around town, or featured in local magazines and newspapers, can aid word of mouth advertising.
  - Posting ads in local magazines and newspapers may cost extra, but it may help to boost your exposure, particularly in smaller communities.
  - Take advantage of putting ads in local periodicals and realtor magazines as these usually provide their readers with additional information about neighborhoods.
- **Podcasts and Other Methods**
  - You may also consider reaching out to local or regional podcasts or confrences to speak about your business, or the consignment business model. The more people you talk to, the more interest you can drum up about your operation.
  - Think about local events happening in your community and whether your business can be of service. This can form strong and reciprocal relationships in which you engage in fund-raising activities or other community events to market your respective businesses together.

Finding Local Producers:

1. **Search your area for local producers** (See *Community Demographics*).
   a. Visit local farmers markets and their websites as there are often lists of vendors you may be interested in working with.
   b. Identify local Community Supported Agriculture (CSA) farms.
2. **Embed yourself in the local food community.**
   a. Attend events that local food enthusiasts attend and get to know prominent people within the local and regional food scene. For example, find out if your community has connections with local farmer's market groups, regional food conferences, and other local food organizations.
3. **Know who are the key local food influencers in your community.**
   a. This helps you understand the dynamics of the local food scene in your area and determine who is best to work with. These people may be farmer's market managers, the heads of local food organizations, or just simply local producers with an active voice in the community. These individuals can point you in the direction of others who would be interested and motivated to work with you, rather than spending time trying to convince those who aren't.

To determine which marketing methods work best for you, consider how you have heard about local businesses opening in your own community, and take advantage of those methods. Lastly, remember to be efficient as marketing can quickly take up a large amount of your time.

Additional Resources: For links to the resources provided on this page, see *Resources, Marketing*.

Related Patterns: Getting Started - Mission, Location - Community Demographics, Financials - Online Store, Operations - Payroll and Staffing, Financials - Producer Relationships

Producer Relationships

Utility: These are your most important relationships because these are the people who will make your store a success! You can't have a Farm Stop without local farmers and producers.

Context: Fostering excellent producer relationships is as important as fostering good relationships with your customers. Never forget that these are the people who prioritize your business.

Assessing Your Needs:

- Before you even seek out producers, consider how many your store can reasonably accommodate, and which types you want to prioritize (see *Physical Space* and *Types of Goods* to understand how to assess this).
  - Considering organizing this via Air Tables (See *Payroll* and *Staffing* for more information)

Finding Local Producers:

1. **Search your area for local producers** (See *Community Demographics*).
   a. Visit local farmers markets and their websites as they often list producers you may be interested in working with.
   b. Identify local Community Supported Agriculture (CSA) farms.
2. **Embed yourself in the local food community.**
   a. Attend events that local food enthusiasts attend and get to know prominent people within the local and regional food scene. For example, find out if your community has connections with local farmer's market groups, regional food conferences, and other local food organizations.
3. **Know who are the key local food influencers in your community.**
   a. This helps you understand the dynamics of the local food scene in your area and determine who is best to work with. These people may be farmer's market managers, the heads of local food organizations, or just simply local producers with an active voice in the community. These individuals can point you in the direction of others who would be interested and motivated to work with you, rather than spending time trying to convince those who aren't.

Contacting Local Producers

Reach out to producers directly.

1. Follow them on social media; visit their website, store and/or farm if they're open to the public. Take the time to learn about who they are and what they do. Call them, email them, or visit them at a non-busy hour at the farmer's market. If possible, tour their property and ask them questions to get acquainted.
2. Your research may include purchasing their products to understand their quality, labeling and packaging.

Establish connections

1. Open opportunities to get to know each other.
2. These initial conversations and meetings help establish trust and rapport, which can then allow you to pitch your idea and gauge their level of interest.

Pitching Your Idea

Contact them:

1. Consider targeting the most influential producers first. If they like the idea, they can recommend it to others.
2. Call, email or visit their property to set up a meeting with the owner(s). Explain that you would like to work with them.
3. Set up a reasonable meeting place and time. Respect their schedule and time as local producers are very busy.

Start a Conversation:

1. Before diving into a presentation, frame the meeting as a conversation.
2. Take time to learn about what they are looking for in additional sales outlets. This is a two-sided relationship so it is important to understand their needs, and if an additional outlet is of interest to them.
3. The more questions you ask, the more you can position your presentation to suit their needs

Present Your Store's Model:

1. **Prepare a brief, but clear, presentation** that covers exactly what your mission and business plan are, and how your store will impact the producer. Test this presentation on friends and family first before you make your first call.
2. **Explain the consignment model,** and what it might potentially look like in your community. If the producer is on the fence about the model itself, here are some positive ideas you can include in your presentation:
   a. Producers receive a much higher amount of money per transaction.
   b. This is a mutual relationship! Your store will prioritize them and their products, and wants them to succeed.
   c. Producers save time and money not going to farmers markets, or other direct-to-consumer outlets; but if they enjoy working with farmers markets, or have other direct-to-consumer outlets, emphasize that the model supports these outlets, instead of competes with them.
   d. Emphasize that your commitment is to market their product! Some stores are able to provide sales and marketing support for producers via social media or internal and external signage, especially at the register. For example, you can advertise via social media when a producer drops off a specialty crop, such as asparagus.

3. **Know the demands of local farmers markets** and other local outlets from the farmer's perspective.
    a. Many farmers don't calculate the actual costs of attending a market. Knowing that a farmer may spend, for example, 20-30% of their revenue from a farmer's market in loading, transportation, staffing, and time away from the farm allows you to make the case for this consignment model as an additional source of revenue for them.

4. **Be concise, organized and clear on your goals.**
    a. State exactly what is required of the producer.

5. **Take frequent breaks**, especially since you're providing a lot of information.

6. **Read the room!** Don't push too hard.
    a. If the producer is distracted or doesn't appear to be listening, don't push them. Offer to reach out at a later point in time.

7. **Leave plenty of time for questions and discussion.**
    a. Ensure that this will be a collaborative process, and that you welcome and respect their feedback. Most people are generally happier when they feel heard, and are invited to participate in a discussion.

8. **Leave them with resources**, contact information, and time to think things over.
    a. But don't overwhelm them! Keep this short and simple.
    b. Unless they are sure of their decision right then and there, chances are they are going to want time to think. Allow this, and reach out to them at a later date to gauge their interest. Don't pressure them!
    c. If they seem enthusiastic, ask them to reach out to other producers they know who may be interested.
    d. Remember, your producers are your greatest resource for word-of-mouth advertising!

Onboarding the Producers: If the producer is ready and willing, walk them through the following processes. Feel free to use this page as a checklist.

☐ **Signing Up:**
  1. Send them a copy of your Producer Application (See *Producer Information in Operations*). Make sure this is a PDF document so they cannot alter information. Use a fillable PDF if sent via email.
  2. Include a discussion of the consignment ratios on the first page to ensure they understand the details.
  3. Give them an overview of what payout reports will look like if you are generating them (See *Resources - Payout Process* for a sample sales report). Have a dry run ready to present as a sample. Note that these reports wil differ based on the Point of Sale System you choose to work with.

☐ **Store Ordering and Delivery:**
  1. Discuss how much product they can provide, and how much you are able to display and store.
  2. Discuss how they package and deliver their goods (ex. Is it delivered in the form they want it displayed?) Ask them for tips on the best display methods for their products.
  3. You may want to discuss additional products you need in the event the producer is willing to expand their offerings.

☐ **The Payout Process:**
  1. See *Payout Process* under Operations. Be sure to explain this well and make sure they understand how this process works within your specific store.

☐ **Dropping Off Goods:**
  1. Provide them with a proposed layout of the space, including access to loading docks, indoor and outdoor storage, as well as parking.
     a. It is recommended to give them a form that ensures they have proof of delivery. See *Resources - Producer Intake Form.*
  2. Decide on a schedule: weekly, biweekly, monthly drop-offs.
  3. Keep this information in an organized space that all staff have access to (Consider Excel or Air Tables. Stay away from paper documents if possible.)
  4. Each time a producer drops off their goods is an opportunity for you to check in with them, learn what's going on with their operations, and assess their experience thus far.

☐ **Operational Aspects:**
  1. Have an internal plan for managing inventory and product display, but communicate this with your producers so you know their preferences.

☐ **Communication:**
  1. Establish formal and reliable methods of communication via phone, email, or other means.
  2. Establish how often you would like to communicate: weekly, biweekly, monthly etc.

Additional Resources: For resources mentioned on this page, See *Resources, Producer Information*

Related Patterns: Getting Started - Mission, Location - Community Demographics, Location - Physical Space, Operations - Payout Process, Operations - Producer Profiles, Operations - Hours and Availability, Operations - Types of Goods, Financials - Community Partnerships, Financials - Business Structure, Financials - Wholesale Options, Financials - Consignment Ratios

OPERATIONS

Operations

Overview: This section provides a broad overview of some of the most important and necessary elements for operating a Farm Stop. You'll notice that this section does not focus predominantly on the physical structure of your store, but rather the inner workings that will help to keep things running smoothly for you, your staff, and your customers. This section primarily relates to understanding the many facets of maintaining energetic and efficient staffing, how a good point of sale system will save you time, money and energy, and how you can keep track of those producer relationships you've been working so hard to develop. This section also covers how to set your hours and availability, and how best to orient your store's layout to ease customer and staff experiences.

Table of Contents:

Payroll and Staffing

Utility: The best thing for your organization to spend time on is staffing and hiring as finding the right people for your store will lead to a greater chance of success.

Context: How you would like to prioritize your staffing structure is highly dependent on the needs of your store, so it is important to understand how many people you can afford to employ based on your projections, and to carefully consider your hours, the length of shifts, and necessary breaks. In addition, you need to understand the hiring practices and wages within your community (See *Community Demographics*). Farm Stops are dynamic; your store's staffing needs may take time to develop and will change as you figure out what works best for you.

Before you even start the hiring process, you will first need a manager. This person should be in charge of hiring, and is the person your employees report to with questions and updates.

The Hiring Process

This is the moment you get to decide what values you are looking for in your ideal candidates, and how you want to structure the process. Do you want to have just one interview? Two? Do you want to vet them first by allowing them to work a few shifts before making your final decision? You get to decide!

For example, the Argus Farm Stop in Ann Arbor, MI goes through a process of two in-person interviews where the candidate meets different team members, and answers different questions that address the following criteria:
- Can they clearly articulate a genuine interest/curiosity in local food?
- Are they genuinely joyful in handling customer service? If not, what tasks are they genuinely interested in doing?
- Does their availability match the store's needs? Will they remain with your store for an acceptable length of time?

Consider the following ideas in selecting your ideal candidates:
- The specific needs of your store (think of all aspects!)
- The store culture you want to create
- The level of customer service experience you want to offer
- The operational complexity of your store
- The range of personalities needed to communicate with all producers and customers

Staffing Basics

It is likely that you will be hiring part or full-time employees before you are profitable. As a general guide, when first starting out, and if you have the resources available, hire someone for the following full-time positions. If you do not have the resources available to hire all positions listed when first starting out, consider ways you can combine job duties to suit the number of roles you can afford.

Store Manager*

- Manages everyone on shift
- Cross-trained and actively working in both market and other aspects of the Farm Stop (ex. Café, community space, kitchen, etc)
- Communicates across shifts
- Keeps a pulse on store energy

Produce Staffer

- Communicates with producers
- Oversees receiving product
- Oversees/maintains displays
- First-responder to market needs (ex. If product runs out, and is in high demand, the Produce Manager will communicate with producers)
- Manages market staff

Payout Staffer

- Coordinates administrative skills to complete payout for all producers (See *Operations - Producer Payout* for more information)

Payroll Staffer

- Coordinates administrative skills to complete payroll for all employees

Marketing Coordinator

- Ensures all marketing materials align with your mission
- Manages and updates all marketing channels (See *Marketing* for more information)

*See *Resources - Payroll and Staffing* for an example description of this role.

Depending on your hours, it is likely you will have two shifts in a day. Have at least two staffers on site for each shift. Keep in mind that if you have a café or other diversified revenue, you will have to hire separate staff. Again, consider the necessary skill sets for all aspects of your store.

Cross-Training

This is a lifesaver for many Farm Stops. One of the biggest opportunities you have here is to have talented staff who can support each other. Farm Stops are dynamic places that deal with many moving parts during the day. Having just one person responsible for one specific task may sound like a good idea, but if that person becomes unavailable, and they are the only one trained in their specific task, you'd be hardwired to find someone else to fill in in a pinch! It may often be the case that you may be able to fill that position yourself, but that takes time away from other organizational or administrative tasks you may need to do.

Table 15: Suggested Starter Roles

Full Time	• Store Manager • Produce Manager • Kitchen/Café Manager (if your store has a deli, café, commercial or incubator kitchen) • Café staff (if applicable)	
Part Time	• Market Staff • Café Staff • Kitchen Staff • Inventory Management • Retail Market Associates • Marketing and Outreach Coordinator	• Human Resources Manager • Accountant • Operational Staffer (to assist when the freezer inevitably decides not to work, or the espresso machine is jammed) • Staff Training Manager
Volunteer	• Market Staff • Café Staff • Kitchen Staff • Inventory Management	

Note: Part-time and Volunteer positions can be interchangeable, but both require the same level of training. Many existing Farm Stops start out relying on volunteers, then move to part-time staff, before finally hiring a team of full-time employees. When working with volunteers, keep in mind that it often takes extra effort to train, manage and keep volunteers.

Regardless of the status of their position, ALL employees should be familiar with the following:
- All equipment and inventory systems
- All Standard Operating Procedures (SOPs)
- Food Safety Rules
  - If you have an on-site commercial kitchen, it is required by law that employees be trained in Food Safety and Handling. Check your local health department to know which specific certifications are necessary.
- Communication systems

Establishing a Consistent Schedule

Establishing a consistent staffing schedule is a challenge to opening any business. The benefit in having a mission is that, ideally, you have employees who are dedicated to your mission and will likely feel a stronger bond to the organization. This may make it easier to establish a consistent schedule.

If you are in an area of seasonality, you may have heavier staffing needs during certain seasons. This means hiring a larger staff during peak times of the year such as the summer months, when local produce is most available, and during the holidays (November-December), when most consumers are looking for fresh, local produce, goods and gifts for their holiday celebrations.

If your store is located in a busy college town such as Wooster, Ohio like Local Roots; or, Ann Arbor, Michigan like Argus Farm Stop, you can take advantage of the opportunity to hire students during the academic year or the summer.

Lastly, identify someone on your staff who can help you with human resources. This individual can help to coordinate schedules and minimize staff turnover to enhance consistency.

Scheduling and Organization:

Scheduling shift work is complicated, especially with part-time, seasonal workers. Luckily, there are many tools available to help organize this task. Consider also creating a uniform method of communication for you and your team. This ensures you have an easy way to post updates and announcements, and to encourage your staff to effectively communicate both on and off shift.

The following is a list of organizational tools to help book and manage shifts. Please note that this is not an exhaustive list. There are many more tools available to aid in organizing workflow, scheduling, training and communication:

- **Humanity**
- **WorkTime**
- **When I Work**
- **Shiftboard**
- **Sling**
- **Calendly**

Training and Store Culture

Training your employees in all aspects of your business is crucial. Consider putting together an employee training manual for new hires. See *Resources - Payroll and Staffing* to request a copy of Argus Farm Stop's Employee Handbook as an example of a training manual. When training your staff in new areas, be sure to pair them with someone more experienced, and to set firm and clear expectations.

Lastly, make sure all employees have access to emergency lists of contacts for troubleshooting technology and machinery. These lists may contain contact information for the Point of Sale (POS) company, maintenance professionals, internet providers, or passwords used around the store.

Here are some important areas in which staff should be well-trained:

Operating Systems

Accessing and using the POS system on the register, card readers, phones, internet, and any other technological tools around the store.

Backup Systems

This is crucial for when your POS system is not working properly.
See *Point of Sale* for ideas about backup systems.

Machinery and Appliances

For those with cafés or commercial kitchens, this includes but is not limited to:
- Espresso/coffee machines
- Toaster ovens and other cooking appliances
- Refrigerators/freezers
- In-store thermostats

Likewise, employees should be trained as far as making in-house fixes, and should know when it's time to call in a professional.

Inventory

All staff should know how to take inventory, and how to receive goods from producers. This also includes keeping track of small-wares in the store such as toilet paper, soap, shopping bags, hand sanitizer etc.

Food Safety and Knowledge

All staff should be trained in standard Food Safety and Operating procedures.

Different states require different food-handling certifications (such as **ServSafe**). At least one person in the store should be certified, but it's best to encourage all employees to get certified. Be sure to check your state Health Department for more information on required certifications.

Company Culture

Monthly staff meetings, bi-annual check-ins, clear communication paths, and a human approach to conflicts are necessary and useful in navigating a highly dynamic environment.

Onboarding Shifts

These are essential to training your staff in all aspects of your operations.

Additional Resources: For links to the resources provided on this page, see *Resources - Payroll and Staffing*

Related Patterns: Operations - Point of Sale, Operations - Producer Payout, Communication - Marketing, Location - Community Demographics

Point of Sale

Utility: Point of Sale (POS) is a fancy way of saying, "cash register." Your Point of Sale is a system, typically owned or licensed by a third party, that facilitates all store transactions (credit card, cash transfer, or plain ol' cash) and also provides important data and metrics on your store's financials. **You cannot get by without a solid, stable point of sale system.**

Context: This is because your POS not only facilitates all store transactions, but it also helps manage your inventory, track which producers' goods sold, and how much you owe that producer according to your consignment ratio.

A POS system for a Farm Stop needs to support selling under consignment where the items in the store are owned by the farms, and not entered into inventory. With this system, it is critical to have the ability to export transaction level data to calculate farmer payouts. Thus, a good POS system will provide you with biweekly, monthly, and/or yearly sales reports that you can share with each individual producer on a set schedule so they know how well their product sells, and whether they need, or want, to produce more or less for your location. Make sure someone in your store understands and is responsible for generating producer payouts. See *Producer Payout* to learn how to facilitate payment via POS systems.

In order to provide accurate data to tell you how much to pay which producers, most POS systems can provide you with bar-codes that you can print and stick onto any and all products. When scanned, these bar-codes tell you exactly which products sold from which producers, and how much money to pay them.

Lastly, POS systems are important if you include an online store as part of your business. Choose a system that integrates with both in-person and online sales.

Here are four popular third-party POS systems used by some existing Farm Stops:
- **RetailEdge**
- **Shopkeep by Lightspeed**
- **Square**
- **Cayan** (note this is a credit-card processor, and not a POS system. This may still provide useful equipment to install alongside your POS system)

If paying for a third-party service like those mentioned above is not accessible at the moment, other stores have created their own. They did this by integrating spreadsheets with DropBox, or by generating new software for themselves. This takes some skill and know-how, and may require hiring or seeking out someone with expertise in software development.

Caveats:

- POS systems can often be finicky, and reliant on good internet access. Be sure you have a strong internet connection, and that you have the company's phone number or emergency hotline available to all employees.
- If your POS system goes down, have alternative systems to process transactions, and make sure you have a fast and easy method of informing your customers of any quick pivots you may need to make to accommodate these alternative systems.
- Make sure your POS system can integrate with SNAP/EBT or other social programs.
- Adding barcodes and stickers to each item is often time consuming, and may require additional staff. It also requires an accessible and working printer. Some stores choose not to spend the time adding the barcodes to each item directly, and instead leave a stack of barcodes next to each item for customers to take and attach for themselves.

Identifying and Linking Products to Producers:

There are a few options to consider when identifying producers with products in your POS system.

- First, consider how the product is sold (ex. By the quart, pound, bunch etc.). This helps to determine the best option for linking that product with its producer.
- For example, if using stickers containing a barcode, consider:
  - Will the sticker get wet?
  - Will a sticker fit the shape of, and stick to, the item?
- You can choose from any of the following options to link products to producers:
  - Barcodes left next to the item
  - Stickers containing a barcode
  - Numbers, using a sticker-gun, that pertain to a barcode
  - Barcodes on pre-packaged items (ex. Coffee or egg cartons)
- Your POS software will likely provide you with a unique barcode for every item that contains a unique 6-digit code. Use this code to label products to keep track of sales for each producer.

If you do not want to place the barcodes on each item yourself: **you must provide clear and visible signage with instructions around the store informing your customers to add a barcode to each item!** Ensuring your customers understand the barcode system will save you a lot of headaches at the register.

Additional Resources: For links to the resources provided on this page, see *Resources, Point of Sale.*

Related Patterns: Operations - Producer Payout, Financials - Social Programs: SNAP/EBT, Financials - Online Store, Operations - Payroll and Staffing

Types of Goods

Utility: Farm Stops prioritize connecting consumers with small-scale farmers and producers, which means they typically carry produce, meat and dairy. Many choose to also offer a wider range of local goods and products. For example, some incorporate artisan products, such as homemade housewares, art, and gifts as additional diversified revenue. Others prioritize offering value-added products, prepared foods, and dried goods. Finally, some stores have branched out to incorporate non-local products like food and household staples. Remember, offering non-local products may add complexity to your operations, and must align with your mission.

Table 16: Here is a non-exhaustive list of goods you may want to offer:

Value-Added/ Prepared Foods	• In-house ready made meals and snacks (See *Sources of Additional and Higher Margin Income*) • Meals and snacks prepared by local restaurants (see *Community Partnerships*) • Jam	• Jelly • Hot sauce • Tomato sauce • Nut Butters • Hummus/dips • Fermented foods (ex. Sauerkraut, kimchi, etc.) • Popcorn
Dried Goods	• Pastas • Grains • Rice • Flours	• Legumes • Oils • Vinegars
Non-Local Products	**Non-local produce:** • Lemons • Avocado • Bananas • Oranges	**Non-local housewares:** • Cleaning supplies • Toilet paper • Paper towels • Personal hygiene • Toothpaste, Soaps, Shampoos, Conditioners
Artisan Products	• Soaps • Pottery • Candles • Decorative Artwork	• Woodwork items • Handmade clothing • Knick-knacks and gifts

72

Important Considerations:

- Your staff must have a strong understanding of the types of goods your store offers, and which producers they came from. This not only helps with organization, but also with sales if customers have questions about specific products.
- The types of goods you offer should be well represented both on store shelves, in back stock, and in your Point of Sale System. See *Point of Sale* to learn of specific platforms that can help you integrate this information. Some Farm Stops use platforms such as **Airtable** to help manage inventory and keep track of which types of goods are offered.

Additional Resources: For links to the resources provided on this page, see *Resources - Type of Goods*

Related Patterns: Financials - Sources of Additional and Higher Margin Income, Financials - Community Partnerships, Communication - Producer Relationships, Operations - Payroll and Staffing, Operations - Point of Sale, Getting Started - Mission

Hours and Availability

Utility: Your hours and availability lets customers know when you're open and accessible, and influences your staffing needs and producer drop-off times. When setting the hours and availability for your store, know that they must reflect consumer demand as well as staff availability. Hours and availability vary widely across existing Farm Stops.

Context: Many existing Farm Stops operate anywhere between five and seven days a week, often with shorter weekend hours. Some stores remain open for six hours a day, others as long as 12. Both have their advantages and disadvantages. For example, keeping your store open seven days a week may bring in more customers, especially when you operate a café or commercial kitchen; but, it does require a tighter staffing schedule as you need more people to manage the store. Likewise, keeping your store open five days a week might alleviate staffing stress, but you may find that you need to make more sales so you can pay your existing staff.

When setting your hours, be mindful of perishable items that depend on your hours of operation. The longer your hours, the more chances there are to sell those goods while they are still fresh and reduce potential food waste.

Producer drop-off:

Many Farm Stops allow producers to drop off whenever is most convenient for them. But some producers may specify the times and dates they will stop by. This requires establishing strong individual relationships with each producer, as well as strong methods of communication such as text, phone call, or email. Ensure you have well-trained staff on hand at all times who understand producer drop-off protocols. Having well-trained staff on hand to assist in producer drop-offs not only helps to collect additional information about the products, which aids in marketing; but it also helps producers gain confidence and trust in your operations.

Here are some things to consider when receiving product:
- Treat product gently and kindly.
- Some food must come at a safe temperature.
- Prepared foods must come labeled.
- Don't leave time and temperature sensitive products out for too long.
- Get clarity from the producer on pricing and quantity (ex. by the pound? quart?)
- Have a copy of the producer's intake form whether they want it or not.
- Make sure all items are properly labeled and recorded BEFORE storing.
- Consider using organizational tools such as **Airtable** to help streamline the process.

See Resources - Producer Relationships for Argus Farm Stop Intake Form as an example of how to record received produce.

74

Standardize your hours:

Standardizing your hours throughout the week and weekend is a good way to reduce customer confusion as well as scheduling conflicts. If your hours are too variable, people may have a hard time finding you when you're open, and feel frustrated that they can't access your services. It also may be harder to establish a regular staffing schedule. Make sure that the correct hours are represented on all places and platforms your business is listed.

Café and Kitchen Hours:

If you have a café or a commercial kitchen, you can choose to have varying hours for each. Just be sure to communicate the difference in hours to your community. For example, your store may be open on Fridays from 8am to 5pm, but your café is open only from 8am to 2pm.

Communicate about your Hours:

People are not going to know you are open unless you tell them! Think about the wide range of people you have to communicate with, and the platforms you are communicating on. Make sure to inform both your producers and also your customers of your hours.

If you need to change your hours, make sure these updates are made on all platforms your business is listed. These can include: your website, Google Business page, Facebook business page, Instagram and other social media, and any local papers, magazines, city guides and online listings.

Here is a sample of how Argus Farm Stop in Ann Arbor, Michigan lists their hours via Google Business, including specific holidays and vacation periods.

Holidays:

While holiday seasons are often a busy time for Farm Stops, be sure to schedule in a seasonal or holiday break, or designate days off for yourself, your staff and your producers! It is up to you to determine how you would like to alter or change the hours of your store to accommodate national holidays such as Thanksgiving.

Google Business Profile Manager

Sunday	8:00 AM–8:00 PM	
Monday	8:00 AM–8:00 PM	
Tuesday	8:00 AM–8:00 PM	
Wednesday	8:00 AM–8:00 PM	
Thursday	8:00 AM–8:00 PM	
Friday	8:00 AM–8:00 PM	
Saturday	8:00 AM–8:00 PM	

More hours
Add hours

12/24/16	8:00 AM–3:00 PM	
12/25/16	Closed	
12/31/16	8:00 AM–3:00 PM	
1/1/17	Closed	
11/23/17	Closed	
7/4/18	8:00 AM–3:00 PM	
9/3/18	8:00 AM–3:00 PM	
4/21/19	8:00 AM–3:00 PM	
9/2/19	8:00 AM–3:00 PM	
12/24/19	7:00 AM–3:00 PM	
12/25/19	Closed	
12/31/19	7:00 AM–3:00 PM	
1/1/20	Closed	
11/25/20	8:00 AM–5:00 PM	
11/26/20	Closed	

Figure 3: Sample of Argus Farm Stop's business hours via their Google Business Profile

Last Minute Changes

Life is unpredictable, and we can't always plan for things. There will be moments when you have to spontaneously change your hours, whether you're experiencing mechanical or technical glitches, problems with the building, weather, or staffing issues. Be sure to clearly and quickly communicate any change in hours to your community and your producers. This is easily done with a quick post to social media, through your website, or even via signage on the door. Contact your producers directly using preferred methods of contact (phone, email, text etc.)

Ultimately, finding the right combination of availability that both sustains your finances and also serves your staffing needs is a delicate balance that takes time.

Here is a breakdown of the availability of existing Farm Stops:
Note the variability for weekdays and weekends, as well as differences in café vs. store hours.

Argus Farm Stop, MI
Monday – Friday: 8am-7pm
Saturday & Sunday: 8am-6pm

The Wild Ramp, WV
Monday – Friday: 9am-6pm
Saturday: 9am-5pm
Sunday: 10am-4pm

Random Harvest, NY
Closed Monday and Tuesday
Wednesday – Sunday: 11am - 6pm

Local Roots, OH
Market Hours:
Monday – Friday: 9am-6pm
Saturday: 8am-5pm
Sunday: 10am-3pm

Café Hours:
Breakfast: Saturday: 8am-11am
Brunch: Sunday: 10am-1pm
Lunch: Monday - Saturday: 11am-2pm

Boone Street Market, TN
Monday - Friday: 10am - 6pm
Saturday: 9am - 5pm
Closed Sunday

Additional Resources: For links to the resources provided on this page, see *Resources - Hours and Availability*

Related Patterns: Operations - Payroll and Staffing, Communication - Marketing, Communication - Producer Relationships

Payout Process

Utility: This represents the schedule of how often you pay your producers, and is likely linked to your Point of Sale system (POS). Payments can be made electronically via direct deposit through your POS, via printed checks or cash mailed directly to your producers, or held at the store for pick-up. This process should be highlighted somewhere in your Producer Application (See *Producer Information* for a sample Producer Application). Make sure that you appoint specific staff member(s) to organize and coordinate payments.

Context: Many Farm Stops follow a bi-weekly payout schedule where producers receive two checks monthly, as well as a sales report to indicate their progress at the store (See *Resources - Payout Process* for an example sales report). Make sure this works for your producers as well. Some stores choose to allow one or two producers to receive just a monthly check, while other producers may need the money sooner depending on their personal financial situation. It is up to you whether or not you are willing to accommodate specific scenarios, but try not to accommodate too many requests as this creates more work, and often more confusion. As a general rule, it is best to unify and automate this process so your producers know exactly when to receive payment and sales reports, and so that you do not need additional staff to manage the payout process every two weeks.

Key Tips:

- Make sure that you have clearly defined and communicated this process with your producers, and that you give them options for their preferred method of payment: direct deposit, mailed check/cash, or in-store pick-up of check/cash.
- Ensure that your staff is well-trained, and that at least one staffer is available to facilitate this process every two weeks.
- Keep your sales data as clean as possible. Errors can often occur when inputting items at the register.

Sales Reports:

It is important that you include a sales report with every paycheck generated for your producers. This lets producers know how much and which of their products are selling, and can indicate sales progress over time. These reports are generated by your POS (See *Point of Sale* for additional information), which usually can automate the process. Keep in mind that sales reports generated by third-party POS systems may look different depending on the system you use. In addition, some POS systems allow you to customize the parameters that are shared with your producers. For example, you may want to show them weekly sales of one particular product, how many times an item was returned, how many weekly transactions occurred etc. See *Resources - Payout Process* for a sample Sales Report from Argus Farm Stop in Ann Arbor, MI. Some stores, such as Local Roots in Wooster, OH and Random Harvest in Craryville, NY have developed online "producer portals" where producers can remotely sign into an account to check the status of their inventory and sales.

Additional Resources: For resources provided on this page, see *Resources - Payout Process*

Related Patterns: Operations - Point of Sale, Operations - Producer Information, Operations - Payroll and Staffing, Communications - Producer Relationships

77

Optimizing Store Layout

Utility: The way you set up your store impacts many aspects of your operations. It directly and indirectly impacts how your customers shop in, and experience, your store. It impacts staff flow, and their ability to stock goods and create a visually appealing display. For example, a disorganized produce or meat shelf will not entice customers to purchase produce or meat. They'll get frustrated trying to find what they want, and when they do, they might not be happy with how it looks in the refrigerator or storage bin. Product presentation counts. As a result, it's worth the time to take a minute and consider the best way to optimize your displays.

Context: There are entire studies devoted to optimizing store layouts, many of which involve understanding elements of behavioral psychology and marketing. There are also important considerations to note, such as the location of the bathrooms in your store, and how that may influence your layout. In addition, remember that your store layout has to make sense to both consumers and staffers! What may make sense to the staffers may not make sense to customers, which can make finding certain items difficult for either party (See *Size of Sellable Space* for sample schematics of store layouts)

Helpful Tips for Designing Your Space:

Understand customer flow. This is the number of people that enter your store, and the patterns in which they shop. For example, you may notice that the majority of people turn right on entering your store. This is what is known as a hotspot, and represents an opportunity to create a display that will catch their eye, and encourage them to buy those specific products.

Notice also, if your store has a cafè or deli, whether your customers venture there first. This can help determine the placement of the café in relation to the grocery section, as well the register. Understanding customer flow can also help you determine the best placement for any equipment required for the cafe or produce. For example, Argus Farm Stop in Ann Arbor, MI designed their space to optimize customer flow in a way that would both accommodate café equipment, and also make the produce deck the most impactful display. This then informed them where to place their cash register.

Understanding customer flow can inform you of what products customers seek out first, which direction they typically go when they enter the store, which areas they visit frequently or not at all, and the optimal placement of equipment to enhance customer flow.

Display

Customer flow ultimately determines how you display your goods. There are many different methods to organize the display of goods. Use this handy guide from **Shopify** to help you find the right layout for your store.

Table 17: Once you've settled on your layout, consider the following when organizing displays.

Display Do's	Display Don'ts
• Do group like items together (ex. Produce, meat, dairy etc.) • Do color coordinate. This makes your displays more appealing. • Do group items according to seasonality. • Do group items according to use. For example: • Cooking vegetables: zucchini, eggplant, peppers. • Cooking greens: kale, collards and chard. • Root vegetables: carrots, radishes, and beets. • Salad greens and microgreens. • Do create a display with a wow factor. • Be creative in using popular seasonal produce, such as tomatoes, in the summer. • Do create an illusion of abundance. • Use the mantra, "Pile 'em high, watch 'em fly" • If the display looks half-empty, it looks picked-over, and people lose interest. • Do cross merchandise. • Display items that inherently go well together (ex. Tomatoes, basil and mozzarella; berries and cream). • Do shorten your displays. • Shoot for four-foot high displays so that people can see over them to what else is around the store. This encourages exploration of other products, specifically a colorful, eye-catching vegetable display. • Do encourage last minute buys. • Place grab'n'go and smaller items near the register. • Do keep the space neat and clean.	• Don't scatter items around the store • This causes undue frustration • Don't poorly organize your space. This includes: • Produce bunches and bags facing different directions with no color scheme. This can disorient customers. • No highlighting of what's in season. • No organization of items according to use. This forces shoppers to search longer. • Don't have bland and half-empty displays. • No use of color or abundance. • Don't separate commonly paired items. • Customers may miss the opportunity, or have to search further throughout the store to find these pairings. • Don't make your displays too high. • This cuts off the view of the rest of the store for your customers and can be disorienting (think of classic supermarket-style shelving). • Don't put hot ticket items where they can't be seen. • Don't let your space get messy 

Below are some examples of how some existing Farm Stops organized their displays:

Source: Argus Farm Stop. (n.d). Produce Display. In Argus Farm Stop 3-day online course

Argus Farm Stop, Ann Arbor, MI

Source: Agricole Farm Stop. (2019). Produce Display. In Agricole Farm Stop Patronicity.

Agricole, Chelsea, MI

Source: Kimberly P. Mitchell (2021). Acorn Farmers Market and Café. In Detroit Free Press.

Acorn Farmers Market and Café, Manchester, MI

Source: Lawrence Braun (n.d). Random Harvest Market.

Random Harvest, Craryville, NY

Storage

(See existing entry under *Location, Physical Space*)

Additional Resources: For links to the resources provided on this page, see *Resources - Optimizing Store Layout*

Related Patterns: Location - Physical Space, Operations - Payroll and Staffing, Operations - Types of Goods, Financials - Sources of Additional and Higher Margin Income

Producer Information

Utility: Typically, Farm Stops work with many producers. Some remain active year-round and sell on a consistent basis, others are seasonal. It is useful to generate profiles for each producer to maintain records on who you are working with, and who you have worked with.

If you choose to offer wholesale relationships as well as consignment, maintaining producer profiles also helps to keep track of who's selling on what model.

Context: There are a few ways you can develop and maintain producer profiles. The first is by ensuring that all producers complete a Producer Application, detailed below. The second is by using an organizational tool such as **Airtable**, to collate and streamline the information gained from the Producer Application.

Producer Applications

This document is a way for you to get to know the producer and their preferences, and for both you and the producer to determine whether or not your store is a good fit for each other. Try to store Producer Applications and other records electronically as often as you can. Paper files are time-consuming, easily misplaced, and hard to find on a moment's notice.

The following is an example of a Producer Application taken from the Argus Farm Stop in Ann Arbor, MI. Note how the document is organized, the specific questions asked of the producer, and the specifications for payment and communication. Your Producer Application does not have to look like this. This is merely an example of the way you may want to structure your application so as to better get to know your producers, and to ensure that you are both a good fit for each other.

Related Patterns: Operations - Payroll and Staffing, Operations - Hours and Availability, Operations - Types of Goods, Operations - Optimizing Store Layout, Communication - Producer Relationships, Location - Parking, Location - Physical Space, Financials - Consignment Ratios, Financials - Wholesale Options.

Dear Market Producer,

Thank you for taking the time to submit an application to supply our market! Before filling out the application, there are a few things to keep in mind. These will help you determine if we are a good match for each other.

Argus Farm Stop has 3 main ways we can grow our local agricultural economy:
- Offer food producers an attractive alternative selling channel that will support their continued growth and season expansion, including an online channel from the Packard store.
- Provide consumers with convenient, year-round access to a broad variety of locally produced food
- Create a community of those who care about local food by providing a place

Argus Farm Stop commitments:
- AFS is open 7 days/week, 12 months of the year (excluding holidays)
- AFS seeks to build a mixture of local products attractive to consumers including vegetables, fruits, meat, dairy, grains, artisanal foods, ready-to-eat and non-perishables.
- AFS has a central check out point, taking multiple forms of payment
- AFS has refrigeration equipment for retail displays & limited storage of products
- AFS refreshes and restock produce from available supplies and will communicate sales and inventory supply information to producers
- AFS works with producers to create signage for their store display, including information about their methods of production and farms / facilities.
- AFS pays 75% of gross sales to producers on a twice/month payment schedule.
- AFS operates a café in the store to encourage a sense of community for your customers and to contribute to our business!

Producer commitments:
- Producers will own and set the price for their products.
- Producers will provide a sufficient supply to match demand through deliveries at least once per week for perishable items, and as needed for non-perishable items. Maintaining availability of products is critical for customer satisfaction and returning business. The store has limited cooler and dry storage space which is available for producers to store inventory.
- Producers should communicate how to best display and care for their products in the market. Products that wilt should be located in cooled areas, bagged, in water, etc. All products should be labeled with bar code labels (provided by AFS) before leaving them at the market.
- Communicating with us about how to care for your products is a key to our success!
- Producers will be responsive and will be proactive in communicating changes.
- Producers will authorize Argus to act on their behalf for replacement items and returns.

APPLICATION & SELECTION OF MARKET PRODUCERS
We accept a limited number of producers in each category (vegetables, fruits, meat, dairy, grains, artisanal foods, ready-to-eat and non-perishables). Selections will be made on a rolling basis, based on product mix needed for store, quality and variety of products from producer and a preference for geographic proximity, sustainability and commitment to early and late season production. If approved, you will need to be re-approved for additional items you have not specified.

KEEP THIS SHEET FOR YOUR RECORDS AND RETURN THE REST OF THE APPLICATION

ARGUS PRODUCER APPLICATION 2020

Date submitted: _____

Farm / Business name _____

Contact name(s) _____

Street Address _____

Mailing Address _____

Phone _____ Email _____

Website _____

Preferred methods of communication (texting, mobile, e-mail)

    #1_____ #2_____

Preferred method of **payment** (we recommend direct deposit which is the last page of this form.)
If by check, whom should we make it out to? IS the address the same as above? (**Checks can be picked up only at the Liberty store.**)

_____

We would like to sell at **325 W Liberty** Ann Arbor MI 48103 ☐

We would like to sell at **1200 Packard** Ann Arbor MI 48104 ☐

Please list **products** you would like to sell at the Argus Farm Stop, along with anticipated timing (which months of year). (**For produce, please fill out the grid on the last page instead**):

_____

_____

 # Of store retail display units requested: [Each retail display unit will be assessed a $10/month fee, which could vary based on the amount of shelf space you take and where that space is]

_____ Non-refrigerated produce (*approximately 3' x 3'*)

_____ Non-refrigerated non-produce (*approximately 1' x 3' of shelving*)

_____ Refrigerated produce (*approximately 2' x 2'*)

_____ Refrigerated dairy (*approximately 2' x 2'*)

_____ Freezer (*approximately 2' x 2'*)

Producer information (answer all that apply):

1. What is your story? Please tell us about yourself and your business. When did you start, what is your vision for the next 5 years, what initiatives have you planned? What is your growth plan (other products you see yourself growing/making in the future)?

    _____

    _____

    a. What is the acreage of your farm? _____

    b. What is the acreage under production? _____

2. Where else do you sell your products currently? (List markets, stores)
   _____
   _____

3. **PRODUCE**: What best describes your growing practices. Check applicable boxes:

   ☐ **Certified Organic**   If Certified Organic please attach a copy of your certification

   ☐ **All Natural**   Not certified organic, but using only OMRI approved inputs.

   ☐ **IPM**   Use Integrated Pest Management Practices, may use chemical
                  fertilizer/pesticides/herbicides

   ☐ **Hoop houses**   or other unique growing methods _____

   ☐ **Non-GMO**   Not using GMO products in our goods, feed or seed stock.

4. *Do you use other growing methods that you would like us to understand? If you use any chemicals on your produce, please tell us here.* **Our customers want to know the growing practices of products in our market. We need to be able to answer as if you were here in the market with us!**
   _____
   _____

5. **MEAT**: If you grow animals for meat, please give us a **complete** description of your growing practices. Your meat must be processed in a USDA-inspected facility. This includes:
   a. Feed policies
   b. Feed products
   c. Pasturing habits of your animals
   d. Antibiotic/hormone usage
   e. How many animals do you have?

6. **EGGS**: Please provide information on
   a. What you feed your chickens (contains soy, GMO use, etc.)
   b. Any pertinent information about the breeds?
   c. How they are pastured (barns, hoop houses, pastures, chicken tractors)
   d. What do you want the customer to know about YOUR eggs?
   e. Approximately how many chickens do you have? _____
   f. Are your eggs processed in a facility licensed by MDARD?   YES   NO
   g. If "f" is YES, please attach a license to the application. If "f" is NO, please describe how you package your eggs (in home kitchen, barn room, etc.)

7. **PREPARED FOODS**: Where do you make your products? Where do you source your ingredients? If you prepare in a licensed kitchen, **please attach a copy of the license.**
   _____
   _____

8. All producers must comply with local, state, and federal requirements regarding the production and sale of their products. See the **Producer Guidelines** for a list of the most common permits and licenses required of market producers. Attach copies of all licenses that apply.

9. Argus Farm Stop is not responsible for any loss or damage incurred by producers. It is preferred that producers carry general liability insurance, but it is the responsibility of each producer to insure themselves to the level they feel is appropriate, and indicate their coverage below:

   ____ General liability coverage of $_____ (please provide proof of insurance)

   ____ No general liability coverage

I have read and understand the Argus Farm Stop **Producer Guidelines**, and agree to comply with all Argus Farm Stop requirements. All information in this application is complete and accurate. I recognize that the goal of the Argus Farm Stop is to help me sell my products and understand that this effort to grow the local food system will requires flexibility and cooperation from everyone involved.

Signed _____   Date _____

Anticipated PRODUCE Plan *(feel free to add more items!!!)*

We realize Mother Nature may have a lot to say on this topic, but for planning purposes, it would be helpful if you could indicate with a check the items you anticipate selling at Argus.

		Varieties: This is not a complete list, add yours if not listed	2015						2015					
			Jul	Aug	Sep	Oct	Nov	Dec	Jan	Feb	Mar	Apr	May	Jun
Cooler	lettuce													
	spinach													
	other greens													
	carrots													
	beets													
	turnips													
	asparagus													
	broccoli													
	cauliflower													
	cabbage													
	Raspberries, fruit													
	Herbs													
	other													
Non-cooled	squash, winter													
	squash, summer													
	potatoes													
	tomatoes													
	peppers													
	sweet corn													
	apples													
	pears													
	blueberries													
	peaches													
	blackberries													
	strawberries													
	other													

This form can be filled out if you are approved as an Argus producer. Don't fill it out unless this has been confirmed and you want direct deposit.

Argus Direct Deposit Authorization – Argus Farm Stop L3C

I (we) hereby authorize Argus Farm Stop L3C, hereinafter called "COMPANY", to initiate credit entries and, if necessary, debit correction and adjustment entries to my (our) account at the financial institution listed below, hereinafter called DEPOSITORY. I (we) acknowledge that the origination of ACH transactions to my (our) account must comply with the provisions of U.S. laws and regulations.

Bank
Name_____

Routing &
Transit Number_____   Account
Number_____

Account Type: □ Checking/Draft   □
Savings/Share

This authorization is to remain in full force and effect until COMPANY has received written notification from the signer(s) below of its termination in such a time and manner as to afford COMPANY and DEPOSITORY a reasonable time to act upon it.

Business Name   _____
(Please Print)

Name on Account   _____
(Please Print)

Date_____   Signature(s) _____

Please attach a voided check to this form,
otherwise you will continue to receive printed checks.

*Note: Written credit authorization **must** provide that the receiver may revoke the authorization only by notifying the orginator in the manner specified in the authorization.*

Licensing

Utility: Farm Stops, as well as any other retail food establishment, are required by their state, city and county to have the proper and necessary licensing to remain operational. As a result, licensing is heavily dependent on your state, city or county rules and regulations. You may also need additional licenses for industry-specific aspects of your business. For example, additional licenses are often required to operate a café or commercial kitchen.

Context: Licensing requirements vary widely between states and also between cities. Visit your state, city and county websites to understand which specific licenses are required for your business.

Note that Federal licenses are not typically required to operate a Farm Stop, but may be required if your Farm Stop wants to offer SNAP/EBT benefits.

Common licenses required for Farm Stops include:
- Retail Food Establishment License - State
- Certificate of Occupancy and Building Permits - City/County
- Sale Tax License - State
- Licenses required by the state department of agriculture - State
- Commercial Kitchen License (if applicable) - State, City/County

In addition to licenses, ensure that your store is up-to-date on the building codes for your county or city. This could require the installation of additional facilities such as bathrooms or sinks around your store.

Table 18: The following is a list of licenses existing Farm Stops use to operate:

Argus Farm Stop, MI	The Wild Ramp, WV	Boone Street Market, TN

• Federal:
  • SNAP/EBT license
• State, Michigan Department of Agriculture (MDARD)
  • Extended Retail Food Establishment
  • Food Safety Standard Operating Procedures
  • Sales Tax License
• City of Ann Arbor
  • Certificate of Occupancy
	• Federal:
	  • SNAP/EBT license
	• State:
	  • West Virginia Department of Health and Human Resources Food Establishment License
	  • Alcohol Beverage Control Administration License
	  • Senior Voucher Farmer's Market Program
	  • West Virginia State Tax Department Business Registration Certificate
	• City of Huntington
	  • Certificate of Occupancy
		• State:
		  • Business license
		  • State sales tax exemption (due to non-profit status)
		  • Tennessee Department of Agriculture commercial kitchen inspections

Related Patterns: Financials - Social Programs: SNAP/EBT, Financials - Sources of Additional and Higher Margin Income, Location - Community Demographics, Finances - Community Partnerships

RESOURCES

Resources and References by Pattern

Context References:

1. Alexander, C., Ishikawa, S., & Silverstein, M. (1977). *A Pattern Language* (M. Jacobson, I. Fiksdahl-King, & S. Angel, Eds.). Oxford University Press.

2. Borman, J., Firouzbakht, N., & Vergara, O. (2020, August 27). Impacts of COVID-19 on the U.S. Agricultural Sector. AIRWorldwide. https://www.air-worldwide.com/blog/posts/2020/8/impacts-of-covid-19-on-the-u-s--agricultural-sector/

3. Clapp, J. (2020, May 8). Opinion | Spoiled Milk, Rotten Vegetables and a Very Broken Food System. The New York Times. https://www.nytimes.com/2020/05/08/opinion/coronavirus-global-food-supply.html?searchResultPosition=3&login=email&auth=login-email

4. Johansson, R. (2020, October 13). *America's Farmers: Resilient Throughout the COVID Pandemic.* United States Department of Agriculture. https://www-usda-gov.proxy.lib.umich.edu/media/blog/2020/09/24/americas-farmers-resilient-throughout-covid-pandemic

5. Lakhani, N. (2020, April 2). "A perfect storm": US facing hunger crisis as demand for food banks soars. The Guardian. https://www.theguardian.com/environment/2020/apr/02/us-food-banks-coronavirus-demand-unemployment

6. Lush, T. (2021, April 20). Coronavirus claims an unexpected victim: Florida vegetables. AP NEWS. https://apnews.com/article/understanding-the-outbreak-fl-state-wire-co-state-wire-nm-state-wire-wi-state-wire-53b783eab84efa228fef8a4bbcf55e7e

7. National Agricultural Statistics Service. "2017 Census of Agriculture." United States Department of Agriculture, Apr. 2019.

8. United States Department of Agriculture; Economic Research Service. (2022a, February 4). Farming and Farm Income. United States Department of Agriculture; Economic Research Service. https://www-ers-usda-gov.proxy.lib.umich.edu/data-products/ag-and-food-statistics-charting-the-essentials/farming-and-farm-income/

9. United States Department of Agriculture; Economic Research Service. (2022b, March 17). Food Dollar Series: Quick Facts. United States Department of Agriculture; Economic Research Service. https://www-ers-usda-gov.proxy.lib.umich.edu/data-products/food-dollar-series/quick-facts/

10. Reiley, Laura, and Andrew Van Dam. "Advocates Hoped Census Would Find Diversity in Agriculture. It Found Old White People." *Washington Post,* 13 Apr. 2019, www.washingtonpost.com/business/2019/04/13/advocates-hoped-new-report-would-find-diversity-ag-it-found-old-white-people/. Accessed 29 Nov. 2020.

11. Yaffe-Bellany, D., & Corkery, M. (2020, April 11). Dumped Milk, Smashed Eggs, Plowed Vegetables: Food Waste of the Pandemic. The New York Times. https://www.nytimes.com/2020/04/11/business/coronavirus-destroying-food.html

Mission

Additional resources to help draft mission statements:

- How to Write a Powerful and Effective Mission Statement, Big Commerce: https://www.bigcommerce.com/ecommerce-answers/how-to-write-a-powerful-effective-mission-statement/
- How to Write a Mission Statement, Susan Ward: https://www.thebalancesmb.com/how-to-write-a-mission-statement-2948001
- Writing a Mission Statement, Tim Berry: https://articles.bplans.com/writing-a-mission-statement/
- The Mission Statement as Your North Star, Ari Weinzweig: https://www.zingtrain.com/article/the-mission-statement-as-your-north-star/

Farm Stop Websites

- Acorn Farmer's Market and Café: https://www.acornfarmersmarketcafe.org/
- Agricole Farm Stop: https://www.agricolefarmstop.com/
- Argus Farm Stop: https://www.argusfarmstop.com/
- Boone Street Market: https://www.jonesboroughlocallygrown.org/boone-street-market
- Local Roots Market and Café: https://www.localrootswooster.com/
- Random Harvest: https://www.randomharvestmarket.com/
- The Wild Ramp: http://wildramp.org/

Financials

Funding resources for food-related businesses:

- Funding Sources for Food-Related Businesses (5th Edition) from the Michigan State University Center for Regional Food Systems: https://www.canr.msu.edu/resources/food_business_funding_sources
- Raising Dough, by Elizabeth Ü: https://www.chelseagreen.com/product/raising-dough/

Funding programs and resources for traditionally underserved communities:

- Community Development Financial Institution (CDFI) Locator: https://ofn.org/cdfi-locator
- Healthy Food Financing Initiative: https://www.investinginfood.com/
- Small Business Administration Loans: https://www.sba.gov/funding-programs/loans
- USDA issued grants:
  - LFPP (Local Food Promotion Program): https://www.ams.usda.gov/services/grants/lfpp
  - FMPP (Farmer's Market Promotion Program): https://www.ams.usda.gov/services/grants/fmpp
  - Check back regularly for new opportunities: https://www.ams.usda.gov/

Business Structure

Small Business Administration resources:

- Choosing the right business structure: https://www.sba.gov/business-guide/launch-your-business/choose-business-structure
- Finding Local Agents: https://www.sba.gov/local-assistance
- Michigan Small-Business Development Center: https://michigansbdc.org/
- Registering your business with the SBA: https://www.sba.gov/business-guide/launch-your-business/register-your-business

Consignment Ratios

Estimating Expenses and Consignment Ratios:

INCOME		
Groceries		
Customers / day	estimate customers per day	50
Sales / customer	estimate average sales per customer	$15.00
Sales / day		$750
Gross Sales		$23,250
Cost of goods sold		75% *
Café		
Customer / day	estimate average sales per customer	48
Sales / customer		$6.50
Gross Sales		$9,672
Cost of goods sold		30%
GROSS SALES (Groceries & Café)		$32,922
COST OF GOODS SOLD (Groceries & Café)		$20,339
GROSS MARGIN (Groceries & Café)		$12,583

*Please note that Argus Farm Stop has since changed their consignment ratio from 75 to 70 percent.

This is a simplified model for estimating your expenses and consignment ratios in Microsoft Excel.

To Calculate your Average Sales/Day:

1. Input the number of customers you expect to receive per day, and your anticipated average sale per customer. Note that these numbers are arbitrary according to your store's specific demographics and goals.
2. Multiply the customers/day by the sales/customer to get your average sales/day.

To Calculate your Gross Sales:

1. Take your average sales/day and multiply it by 31 (the number of days in a month). 31 represents the days your store will be open if you plan on operating seven days/week year-round. If you do not plan on operating seven days/week year-round, use the number of days in a month you plan to be open. For example, if you plan to operate your store five days/week, 31 will change to 22 as you subtract the total days you will be closed from the total days in the month (31-8).
2. Do this calculation for each revenue stream in your business.

To Calculate your Total Gross Sales: Add up the Gross Sales from each revenue stream. For example, in this spreadsheet, the Gross Sales for Groceries is $23,250, and $9,672 for the Café. When added together, the total Gross Sales is $32,922.

To Calculate the Cost of Goods Sold: Incorporate the consignment ratio by multiplying the Gross Sales for each revenue stream by the percentage you plan to use for your consignment ratio. For example, in this sheet, $23,250 is the Gross Sales for the Groceries section. This is multiplied by 0.75, which represents the 75 percent consignment ratio for a new total of, $17,437.50. The same is done with the Café, for a new total of $2,901.60. These totals were added to equal $20,339.

To Calculate your Gross Margin for All Revenue Streams: Subtract the total from Cost of Goods sold from the total Gross Sales. For example, in this spreadsheet, The Cost of Goods Sold ($20,339) is subtracted from the Gross Sales ($32,922) for a Gross Margin of $12,583.

Consignment Ratios

Estimating Expenses and Consignment Ratios: The following are sample estimate templates from Argus Farm Stop. Use the top chart to estimate startup expenses, and the bottom chart to estimate total operating expenses

Startup costs	estimate	comments
Architect	$7,500	
Creative	$1,500	interior design
Interior decoration	$5,000	
Accounting	$0	accountant pro bono
Legal	$4,000	L3C setup; lease review;
Website	$250	
Registers / scales / POS	$5,000	
Freezer / refrigerators	$60,000	reconditioned used with new compressors: produce deck, reach in cooler and freezer and 8x10 walk in cooler
Checkout counter	$10,000	
Café setup (all equipment)	$20,000	
Ice maker	$2,000	
Retail displays	$5,000	shelving and display units; found good used ones when opened 2nd store
Signs / awning	$7,500	
painting	$3,500	interior painting up to leasee
store supplies	$2,000	cups, lids, bags, etc.
interior lighting	$3,000	
tables & chairs	$2,000	
hand sink	$500	
mop sink	$500	
3 compartment sink	$200	
plumbing	$10,000	hot water heater needs to meet health dept specifications. Pricey!
electrical	$10,000	our buildings have needed lots of work
flooring	$8,000	
wire racks	$1,000	
storage shed for rear	$4,000	
startup personnel expenses	$14,216	manager for 3 months before opening, rest of staff for 2 weeks before opening
advertising & promotion	$2,000	
Total cash needed before opening day	$188,666	
Cash needed for first 18 months	$20,898	
Total cash needed	$209,564	

Everyday Farmers Market - INCOME STATEMENT		14-Aug
EXPENSES		
Personnel Costs		
Store Manager (1 FTE)	$35,000 per year	2,917
Associates (coffee)	$10 per hour x 12 hours open per day	3,720
Associates (grocery)	$10 per hour x 12 hours open per day	3,720
Payroll & Salary Expense		10,357
Payroll Taxes & Benefits	25% mgr; 10% Assoc	1,473
Total Personnel Costs		11,830
Occupancy Expenses		
Rent		2,500
Liability Insurance	$1,000 per year	83
Repairs & Maintenance	0.4% of gross sales	132
Insurance	0.4% of gross sales	132
Utilities (inc. internet/phone)	$9 per sq ft per year	953
Licenses & Permits	$1,000 per year	83
Total Occupancy Expenses		3,883
Operating Expenses		
Store Supplies	1.25% of gross sales	412
Credit Card Fees	2.0% of gross sales	658
Trash/Baler	$200/month	200
Bad Debt, Bank Charges	0.1% of gross sales	33
Miscellaneous	0.25% of sales	82
Total Operating Expenses		1,385
Total Administrative Expenses		412
Total Promotional Expenses		395
TOTAL OPERATING EXPENSES		17,904
INCOME FROM OPERATIONS		(5,321)

Consignment Ratios

Estimating Expenses and Consignment Ratios:

Use the following Gantt chart from the Argus Farm Stop to get an idea of a potential timeline you can adhere to when building out and opening your store. A Gantt chart is a useful organizational tool that helps to align specific timelines and goals for a project.

Note that the Argus Farm Stop opened within a year of finding a location, securing funding, and building out the store. This does not have to be the case for your store! All existing Farm Stops operate differently, and went through their own, unique timeline to open their stores. This example is meant purely as a suggested template.

Gantt charts often require the use of third-party software. The following is a non-exhaustive list of suggested software:
- Instagantt: https://instagantt.com/
- Team Gantt: https://www.teamgantt.com/
- AirTable: https://www.airtable.com/articles/product/how-to-make-a-gantt-chart

	Nov-13	Dec-13	Jan-14	Feb-14	Mar-14	Apr-14	May-14	Jun-14	Jul-14	Aug-14
Complete Feasability Evalutations	█	█	█	█						
Store Location	█	█	█	█						
Financials	█	█	█	█						
Producer Interest	█	█	█	█						
Zoning/Regulation/Licensing Requirements	█	█	█	█						
Assess Team/Skills Needed	█	█	█	█						
Build Business Plan/Pitch Deck	█	█	█	█						
Commit Financially					█	█	█	█	█	█
Incorporate Business					█	█	█	█	█	█
Raise Money					█	█	█	█	█	█
Build Out Store					█	█	█	█	█	
Sign Lease					█	█	█	█	█	
Select/Hire Store Manager					█	█	█	█	█	
Design Store Layout					█	█	█	█	█	
Construction Drawings					█	█	█	█	█	
Select Contractor					█	█	█	█	█	
Building Permits/MDARD License					█	█	█	█	█	
Sign up Producers					█	█	█	█	█	
Install POS System					█	█	█	█	█	
Get Ready to Open					█	█	█	█	█	
Certificate of Occupancy/MDARD License					█	█	█	█	█	
Hire Opening Staff					█	█	█	█	█	
"Soft" Opening					█	█	█	█	█	

Wholesale Options

Regional Distributors used by existing Farm Stops:

- Argus Farm Stop:
  - Cherry Capital: https://cherrycapitalfoods.com/
  - Frog Holler: https://www.froghollerproduce.com/delivery
- Random Harvest:
  - Hudson Harvest: https://www.hv-harvest.com/
  - Baldor: https://www.baldorfood.com/
  - Associated Buyers: https://www.assocbuyers.com/
  - Farms2Tables: https://www.transparentfood.co/
  - Marty's Local: https://www.martyslocal.com/
  - Regional Access: https://regionalaccess.net/
  - Mable: https://meetmable.com/
- Boone Street Market:
    Southern Culture: https://www.southernculturellc.com/
  - Blue Mountain: https://www.bluemountaindistributors.com/

Funding Mechanisms

Small Business Development Center: https://americassbdc.org/

Grants

List of USDA federal grant programs:

- National Institute of Food and Agriculture: https://nifa.usda.gov/programs#competitive
- Food and Nutrition: https://www.fns.usda.gov/fm/grant-opportunities?page=2
- Agriculture and Marketing Service: https://www.ams.usda.gov/services/local-regional/food-sector/grants

Non-Federal Grants Databases. Be sure to check back often as dates and availability change:

- The National Association of State Departments of Agriculture: https://www.nasda.org/states/state-directory
- Community Foundation Locator: https://www.cof.org/page/community-foundation-locator
- American Heart Association: https://www.heart.org/en/professional/institute/grants
- Candid: https://candid.org/

Additional grant resources:

- Michigan State University Center for Regional Food Systems Funding Sources for Food-Related Businesses: Sixth Edition https://www.canr.msu.edu/resources/food_business_funding_sources

Community Events as Fundraisers

Organizational Tools for Event Planning:

- Mural: https://www.mural.co/
- Miro: https://miro.com
- Trello: https://trello.com/
- Excel Event Planning Templates: https://www.free-power-point-templates.com/articles/free-community-event-planner-template-for-excel/

Donations and Crowd-Sourcing

Crowd-Sourcing websites and resources:

- GoFundMe: https://www.gofundme.com/c/blog/ask-for-donations
- Constant Contact - can integrate with fundraising apps to aid in sending mass emails: https://www.constantcontact.com/features/apps-integration
- Indiegogo: https://entrepreneur.indiegogo.com/education/guides/
- Kickstarter: https://www.kickstarter.com/creators?ref=global-footer
- Patronicity: https://www.patronicity.com/
- 5 Ways to Boost Your Wording When Asking for Donations: https://www.soapboxengage.com/blog/1806-5-ways-to-boost-your-wording-when-asking-for-donations

Free online graphic design platforms:

- Canva: https://www.canva.com/
- Figma: https://www.figma.com/

Loans

Counseling resources for seeking out loans:

- Annual Credit Report: www.annualcreditreport.com
- Credit Karma: https://www.creditkarma.com/
- National Foundation of Credit Counseling: www.nfcc.org
- Small Business Administration: https://www.sba.gov/funding-programs/loans
- Small Business Development Center: https://americassbdc.org/

Additional platforms for raising loans:

- Lending Club - https://www.lendingclub.com/
- Prosper - https://www.prosper.com/home-new
- Kiva - https://www.kiva.org/

Sources of Additional and Higher Income

Subscription Services

Online platforms to facilitate subscription services:

- Shopify: https://www.shopify.com/
- Squarespace: https://www.squarespace.com/ecommerce-website
- Local Line: https://site.localline.ca/
- Barn2Door: https://www.barn2door.com/
- Harvie: https://www.harvie.farm/
- Farmigo: https://www.farmigo.com/
- Mercato: https://www.mercato.com/
- Local Food Marketplace: https://home.localfoodmarketplace.com/
- Square: https://squareup.com/us/en

Educational Classes and Community Events

Tools to aid in Event Planning:

- Event Brite: https://www.eventbrite.com/
- Brown Paper Tickets: https://www.brownpapertickets.com/createevent.html
- Nextdoor: https://nextdoor.com/
- Zoom: https://zoom.us/

Online Store Resources

Online platforms to facilitate online sales:

- Local Line: https://site.localline.ca/
- Barn2Door: https://site.localline.ca/
- Food4All: https://www.food4all.com/
- GrazeCart: https://grazecart.com/
- LocalOrbit: https://localorbit.com/
- Open Food Network: https://www.openfoodnetwork.org/who-we-are/
- Online Farm Markets: https://onlinefarmmarkets.com/
- Shopify: https://www.shopify.com/
  - RetailEdge: https://retailedge.com/
- SquareSpace: https://www.squarespace.com/
- Wix: https://www.wix.com/
- Magento: https://business.adobe.com/products/magento/magento-commerce.html
- WooCommerce: https://woocommerce.com/

SNAP/EBT
Resources to help facilitate incorporation of social programs at Farm Stops:
- Supplemental Nutrition Assistance Program: https://www.benefits.gov/benefit/361
- USDA Food and Nutrition Service: https://www.fns.usda.gov/snap/apply-to-accept
- Retailer Training Materials: https://www.fns.usda.gov/snap/retailer/training
- Retailer Requirements to Provide Online Purchasing to SNAP Households: https://www.fns.usda.gov/snap/retailer-requirements-provide-online-purchasing
- Fair Food Network: https://fairfoodnetwork.org/projects/fair-food-fund/
- Double Up America: https://doubleupamerica.org/
- SNAP Stretch: https://www.snapstretch.com/
  - http://wildramp.org/snap-stretch/

Community Demographics
Online demographic resources:
- US Census Bureau - QuickFacts Tool: https://www.census.gov/quickfacts/fact/table/US/PST045221
- Census Business Builder: https://www.census.gov/data/data-tools/cbb.html
- Small Business Development center: https://www.sba.gov/local-assistance/find?type=Small%20Business%20Development%20Center&pageNumber=1
- DataUSA: https://datausa.io/
- TownCharts: https://www.towncharts.com/
- The American Library Association: https://www.ala.org/rt/magirt/publicationsab/demdata

Communication
Marketing
Popular marketing sites and tools:
- Facebook Business Suite: https://www.facebook.com/business/help/205614130852988?id=765488040896522
- Nextdoor: https://nextdoor.com/
- Google Business: https://www.google.com/business/
- Constant Contact: https://www.constantcontact.com/
- Mailchimp: https://mailchimp.com/

Food-related marketing sites:
- Eat Local Grown: www.eatlocalgrown.com
- Eat Well Guide: www.eatwellguide.org
- Farmer's Market Coalition Directory: www.farmersmarketcoalition.org
- LocalHarvest: www.localharvest.com
- Edible Communities: https://www.ediblecommunities.com/
- Destination Ann Arbor: https://www.annarbor.org/
- Local Small Business Development Centers: https://www.sba.gov/local-assistance/resource-partners/small-business-development-centers-sbdc

Producer Relationships

Intake Form

Producer _____

Label - Store - Retail Edge Maintenance - Barcode – Signage - Display

Item Name & Variety	Quantity (lbs, cases, etc.)	Price per Unit ($/lb, $/ea, $/qt, etc.)	Date Received/ Staff Initials	Notes – What does the producer want to share about this item? Why Grown, Storage/Display Preferences, Potential Uses, etc.

Labels for Processed Items Need:			**Time/Temperature Sensitive Items Must:**
▢ Product Identity			▢ Arrive in Cooler/Refrigerated Unit
▢ Ingredients & Sub-Ingredients			▢ Be at Temperature:
▢ Allergens			▢ Milk/Eggs: $\leq 45°$
▢ Net Weight (both US & Metric)			▢ Prepared Foods: $\leq 41°$
▢ Producer Name & Address			▢ Frozen Items: $\leq 32°$
▢ Best/Sell By date Or Lot Number			

Operations

Payroll and Staffing

Argus Farm Stop Manager position description:

We are seeking a Store Manager to join as a founding member of the Argus Farm Stop team. This person would have a strong commitment to and passion for growing the local food ecosystem, and demonstrate enthusiasm for local food. This person will have a significant impact, and will heavily influence the organization, implementation and operation of the Argus Farm Stop.

Responsibilities

- Management of store operations during scheduled shifts
    - Manage the opening and closing of the store
    - Oversee receipt of deliveries from producers, inventory and restocking
    - Customer relations
    - Oversee merchandising and store organization/cleanliness
    - Manage staff
- Marketing
    - Build awareness for local food and the Argus mission through social media, special events, and other promotional activities.

Skills/Experience

- Must be detail-oriented, with excellent communications and supervisory skills and the ability to handle multiple demands.
- A sincere appreciation and joy in other people and having an ability to maintain a calm demeanor under challenging circumstances are necessary to being successful in this role. Has a desire to lead by example with a grace of authority. Exudes a positive attitude and sustains a contagious energy throughout entire shift.
- Provides a model of supportive and participatory leadership promoting the concepts of team building and empowerment, and experience in hiring and training of new employees
- Customer service orientation to help build a store culture that is warm and inviting to our guests. Takes pride in being a product knowledge expert and communicating with guests about products. Is dedicated to learning from others, constantly shares information and asks questions.
- Experience in working with local producers (produce, meats, dairy, etc.). Knowledge of organic and commercial growing practices as well as organic certification and food safety requirements
- Retail produce and management experience preferred to help direct and maintain inventory, produce mix and merchandising standards. Working knowledge of point of sale systems and accurate cash handling procedures.
- Commitment to working shifts as scheduled and flexibility to work additional hours and/or different hours based on changing needs of the business.
- Possesses strong selling skills, including anticipating the needs of customers and implementing the appropriate action or solution
- Demonstrated desire to manage a mission-driven business

Status

- Full-time, salaried management position
- Compensation commensurate with experience, including 15 days per year of vacation/sick days.

Operations

Payroll and Staffing

Argus Farm Stop Produce Staffer description:

Local Foodivore

Argus Farm Stop is looking for team members who are passionate and deeply committed to Ann Arbor & our local food community. Our top priority is to grow and connect our local food producers to Ann Arbor by providing a great customer service experience for our customers, our producers, and the community. We are looking for efficiency, adaptability, kindness, and passion.

At Argus Farm Stop, customers are able to purchase 100% locally produced and grown produce, meat, dairy and dried goods, every day and year-round. We also offer a full café with coffee from Roos Roast. We see this as a need for the Ann Arbor community. The Farm Stop aims to give farmers an accessible and convenient venue to sell their products and retain their farm's identity. If we can make local foods more accessible daily and year-round to consumers, we will be better able to grow our local food system and improve local food security.

This is an extremely varied position in a new small business, and thus we need team members who are both committed to being dependable and consistent, while remaining flexible and adapting to new needs in the market. This position spans many different activities and team members must be able to work actively, not passively. We believe that one of the core elements to this model being successful in Ann Arbor is to provide wonderful customer service.

Essential job functions:

- Willingness to be cross-trained as a barista, grocer, cashier and advocate.
- Act with the integrity, honesty & knowledge that promote the culture, mission and values of Argus Farm Stop.
- Maintain a calm and upbeat demeanor that promotes a positive work environment during times of high volume, stress or unusual events.
- Anticipate guest and store needs by frequently evaluating the environment.
- Realize that actions & inactions are magnified in this small environment and act accordingly. Consistently maintaining an eye for detail throughout all activities.
- Follow Argus-set and food safety protocols in regards to cash handling, food handling, drink making, food safety and security.
- Strong ability and willingness to identify with and communicate the individuality of different products. Our producers are very proud of their work, and the handling of their products must reflect this.
- Being an advocate for our local producers and local food economy, and having an interest in learning & education.
- We are a neighborhood store, and need a staff who recognize neighbors, and are warm and friendly.

Scheduling

- Humanity: https://www.humanity.com/
- WorkTime: https://www.worktime.com/
- When I Work: https://wheniwork.com/
- Shiftboard: https://www.shiftboard.com/
- Sling: https://getsling.com/
- Calendly: https://calendly.com/

Training and Store Culture

Employee Handbooks:

- Contact the Argus Farm Stop to ask for a sample Employee Handbook: https://www.argusfarmstop.com/learn; training@argusfarmstop.com

Food Handling Certifications:

- ServSafe: https://www.servsafe.com/

Point of Sale

Point of Sale Platforms:

- RetailEdge: https://retailedge.com/
- Shopkeep by Lightspeed: https://www.lightspeedhq.com/shopkeep/
- Square: https://squareup.com/us/en
- Cayan: https://www.authorize.net/sign-up/reseller-directory/cayan.html

Types of Goods

Inventory Organization Tools:

- Airtable: https://www.airtable.com/

Hours and Availability

See Resources - Producer Relationships for Argus Farm Stop Intake Form

Schedule Organizer:

- Airtable: https://www.airtable.com/

Payout Process

Sales Reports: Sample Sales report from Argus Farm Stop:

Sum of Sale_Items_Price_Extension / Location_Farm Name+Item	Jan	Feb	Mar	Apr	May	Jun	Jul	Aug	Sep	Oct	Nov	Dec	Grand Total
Liberty	$35	$432	$708	$1,341	$633	$701	$2,615	$4,497	$3,329	$2,226	$3,156	$1,523	$21,196
FARM NAME	$35	$432	$708	$1,341	$633	$701	$2,615	$4,497	$3,329	$2,226	$3,156	$1,523	$21,196
FARM_NAME_TOMATOES_HEIRLOOM_GREEN_LB							$1,505	$1,689	$722	$30			$3,946
FARM_NAME_SPINACH_BAG		$432	$525	$707					$132	$72	$848	$216	$2,931
FARM_NAME_LETTUCE_HEAD_EA							$198	$830	$479	$132	$293	$270	$2,202
FARM_NAME_KALE_BUNCH			$183	$635		$5	$72	$99	$367	$299	$219	$140	$2,017
FARM_NAME_CARROTS_BUNCH							$76	$145	$240	$243	$501	$191	$1,396
FARM_NAME_GARLIC_BULB							$216	$235	$48	$224	$163	$209	$1,094
FARM_NAME_ASPARAGUS_LB					$624	$392							$1,016
FARM_NAME_HERBS_BUNCH							$176	$101	$186	$210	$203	$138	$1,013
FARM_NAME_COLLARDS_BUNCH							$80	$64	$64	$84	$176	$143	$611
FARM_NAME_GREEN_BEANS_QUART							$65	$308	$150	$75			$598
FARM_NAME_TURNIPS_BUNCH							$21	$85	$60		$116	$137	$418
FARM_NAME_TOMATOES_CHERRY_PINT							$30	$303	$85				$418
FARM_NAME_SQUASH_SUMMER_LB							$92	$101	$185	$27			$405
FARM_NAME_OKRA_QUART							$50	$230	$94				$374
FARM_NAME_EGGPLANT_LB							$54	$175	$125	$3			$357
FARM_NAME_CORN_EA							$257	$92					$349
FARM_NAME_BEETS_BUNCH							$14	$60	$28	$142	$49		$292
FARM_NAME_CHARD_BUNCH								$11	$161	$46			$217
FARM_NAME_GARLIC_SCAPES_BUNCH					$151		$48						$198
FARM_NAME_ONIONS_GREEN_BUNCH								$75	$9		$114		$198
FARM_NAME_RADISHES_BUNCH										$123	$70		$193
FARM_NAME_TAT_SOI_BAG										$52	$140		$192
FARM_NAME_ARUGULA_BAG										$96	$84		$180
FARM_NAME_LETTUCE_HEAD_BAG					$154	$23							$177
FARM_NAME_CELERY_BUNCH								$40	$66				$106
FARM_NAME_HAKUREI_TURNIPS_LB									$2		$6	$70	$78
FARM_NAME_MUSTARD_GREENS_BAG											$69		$69
FARM_NAME_PEPPERS_HOT_EACH										$22	$16	$4	$42
FARM_NAME_BEETS_LB											$35	$6	$40
FARM_NAME_WINTER_SQUASH	$28												$28
FARM_NAME_PEPPERS_POBLANO_EACH										$10			$10
FARM_NAME_STRAWBERRY_QT					$10								$10
FARM_NAME_PUMPKIN_PIE_LB	$7												$7
FARM_NAME_FLOWERS_BOUQUET										$6			$6
FARM_NAME_DECORATIVE_GOURD_EA											$5		$5
FARM_NAME_CARROTS_LB											$3		$3
FARM_NAME_TOMATOES_SAUCE_LB								$3					$3
Packard		$822	$1,062	$1,224	$511	$531	$2,577	$2,872	$2,339	$2,106	$2,037	$2,164	$18,245
FARM_NAME		$822	$1,062	$1,224	$511	$531	$2,577	$2,872	$2,339	$2,106	$2,037	$2,164	$18,245
FARM_NAME_PINACH_BAG		$822	$1,062	$1,182							$309	$1,709	$5,084
FARM_NAME_TOMATOES_HEIRLOOM_GREEN_LB							$340	$1,182	$293	$7			$1,822
FARM_NAME_SQUASH_SUMMER_LB							$17	$618	$676				$1,311
FARM_NAME_LETTUCE_HEAD_EA							$488	$128	$315	$51	$83	$72	$1,136
FARM_NAME_ARROTS_BUNCH							$448	$300	$156	$191	$18	$14	$1,126
FARM_NAME_EGGPLANT_LB								$465	$630	$3			$1,098
FARM_NAME_BEETS_BUNCH							$403	$44		$553	$77	$11	$1,087
FARM_NAME_TURNIPS_BUNCH							$21	$455	$37		$522	$23	$1,057
FARM_NAME_TOMATOES_1LB							$829	$51					$880
FARM_NAME_KALE_BUNCH							$20	$45	$54	$47	$234	$137	$536
FARM_NAME_ASPARAGUS_LB						$516							$516
FARM_NAME_HERBS_BUNCH				$42	$18		$18	$114	$140	$137		$8	$475
FARM_NAME_LETTUCE_HEAD_BAG					$413	$15			$5	$5			$438
FARM_NAME_GARLIC_BULB										$93	$205	$103	$400
FARM_NAME_COLLARDS_BUNCH								$20	$26	$44	$130	$52	$272
FARM_NAME_CHARD_BUNCH										$100	$47	$7	$154
FARM_NAME_OKRA_QUART									$88	$40			$128
FARM_NAME_GREEN_BEANS_QUART									$53	$40			$93
FARM_NAME_ARUGULA_BAG										$25	$63		$88
FARM_NAME_OPEN_ITEM					$80								$80
FARM_NAME_PUMPKIN_PIE_LB										$29	$27		$56
FARM_NAME_PEPPERS_HOT_EACH										$2	$52		$54
FARM_NAME_HAKUREI_TURNIPS_LB									$23		$5	$22	$49
FARM_NAME_RADISHES_BUNCH							$4			$46			$49
FARM_NAME_TAT_SOI_BAG											$16	$32	$48
FARM_NAME_MUSTARD_GREENS_BAG										$40			$40
FARM_NAME_CORN_EA									$37				$37
FARM_NAME_PEPPERS_LB										$31	$2		$32
FARM_NAME_CARROTS_LB											$23	$3	$26
FARM_NAME_SQUASH_HONEYNUT_LB											$18		$18
FARM_NAME_TOMATOES_SAUCE_LB							$9	$8					$17
FARM_NAME_LEMONGRASS_BUNCH											$9	$3	$12
FARM_NAME_CELERY_BUNCH							$4	$4					$8
FARM_NAME_GARLIC_SCAPES_BUNCH											$7		$7
FARM_NAME_PUMPKIN										$7			$7
FARM_NAME_BEETS_LB											$2	$2	$4
FARM_NAME_ONIONS_GREEN_BUNCH											$3		$3
FARM_NAME_WINTER_SQUASH								$0					$0
Grand Total	$35	$1,254	$1,770	$2,565	$1,144	$1,232	$5,191	$7,369	$5,668	$4,332	$5,194	$3,688	$39,441

Optimizing Store Layout

- The Ultimate Guide to Retail Store Layouts: https://www.shopify.com/retail/the-ultimate-guide-to-retail-store-layouts